Introduction:

I have always enjoyed telling stories. As a teacher, I use this practice a great deal—and for various purposes. When I first started in the profession, it provided a way to connect with colleagues and impart a sense of belonging within the teaching community. Oh, the many stories I have compiled after years of doing this! During one particularly memorable school assembly, Jimmy A. shouted, "F#ck the police! No cell can hold me!" as he sprinted from his seat before swooping into and driving off in the solar panel car that was proudly on display. Recounting this story has formed a special bond amongst the staff in attendance that day. Then, there was the time that Marisa was caught red-handed smoking in the student toilets by a staff member and simply replied nonchalantly, "My doctor prescribed it." Such a calm, cool, and collected response would make even the most seasoned staff member pause momentarily to question the validity of Marisa's excuse, then ponder how much society has changed since they started in the profession way back when.

Over time, I have honed my ability to use these and other stories to paint a picture of what teaching *really* involves to outsiders. Not only do my stories help me walk non-teaching folk through the ins and outs of the daily events and long-term lessons and rewards of teaching, but they act as a behind-the-scenes look at the profession. I have learned the value in finding just the right story to share with the many bozos with whom I have crossed paths who say things like, "You get twelve weeks holiday a year. How hard can it be!?" It always brings a smile to my face when they finally realize the truth. It's a beautiful thing to witness their smug demeanour fade into stark disbelief and embarrassment as they realise just how much is involved in teaching—and playing such a significant role in the lives of young people. I guess, finally, telling these stories may just be my way of processing the day-to-day intricacies of teaching: a way to unwind and make sense of it all. Or, quite frankly, maybe I just need to focus on finding a way to laugh out of fear that otherwise, I will lose myself to insanity.

I had always told myself that at one point, I would start to write these stories down, never really knowing if I would do so. Then, when COVID-19 began, a strange thing happened... Free time became a thing! I seized the opportunity, and I got busy. During this writing period, I had just qualified for my first round of long-service leave. It truly felt like just the other day that I was a fresh-faced graduate heading up to the country to teach. Somehow, I had blinked my eyes and ten years had flown by. The writing process afforded me the wonderful benefit of reliving the many memories I share within the following pages: the characters I have met along the way and the experiences I have had (both good and bad). One thing is for sure: the teaching profession's breadth, depth, and overall complexity never ceases to amaze me.

Let me tell you a little more about me. I am thirty-five years old at the time of writing. I started teaching at twenty-three years old in rural Western Australia, and although I felt like I was mature enough to handle it at the time, in reality, most days, I would constantly remind myself to "fake it till you make it." I thought if I acted confident enough, the students would have no choice but to believe what I said... and that I knew what I was doing. I have always taught high school mathematics in tough schools throughout my teaching career. I did have a stint at a senior campus, and when I tell stories to colleagues, they consider it the gold standard within the profession. Nevertheless, the school did present its own set of difficulties.

Who is this book for? First, it's for anyone considering or about to start teaching. I applaud you! I hope you can learn a thing or two from my trials and tribulations. Second, it's for anyone who has already been teaching for a while. If this is the case, I have one thing to say: You are a star! Sometimes we just need to sit back, have a good laugh, and remind ourselves that these crazy things really *did* (and continue to) happen! Finally, it's for anyone outside of the teaching realm who wonders what actually goes on in the day-to-day life of a teacher. Let me tell you, though, these stories are only the tip of the iceberg. They have nowhere near done the profession justice.

Finally, these stories have been kept short on purpose, as I am always conscious of people's time. I just wanted it to be something you could pick up and quickly find a passage that may help you through your day. Maybe you had a horrific day, and you need some relief. Pick up this book and let me guide you through some of my worst days. Maybe you are sitting at home watching your latest TV series, and suddenly you are reminded that you have the year 9 Dream Team first thing tomorrow. Pick up the book and read about the time I was locked in my classroom while teaching and had to wait an hour for the rescue team to arrive. Maybe within these pages you will find even the smallest amount of help to make your life easier heading forward. If so, I hope you will share that with me as it will surely bring a smile to my face. After all, we are in one of the most challenging professions in the world, so let's make sure we look after one another!

A Day in the Life

It is easy to walk to the staff car park after a particular hard day and think we have had minimal effect on the world. What used to grind my gears even worse was when people outside the profession would tell me teaching can't be that hard: just open your classroom door, take the role, and start teaching. I became so frustrated with having this conversation with people over and over I decided to write down everything I did one day to give a snapshot into the life of a teacher.

- Wake up early to have enough time to complete meditations, visualisations, and prepare my mind for the day. Remind myself that although students may wag class, tell me to get f$$ked, or be disruptive, deep down they want to learn; there is just a lot to this game. Best not to take it personally.
- Hit the road early to beat traffic to arrive at school to finish planning for the day. If you are lucky, you will not have meetings, bus duty, or morning tutorials.
- Arrive to the first class full of motivation, passion, and willingness. Students stumble into class with minimal motivation, passion, and willingness.
- Give initial instructions to begin the lesson only to find half the students in class do not have something to write with, another quarter have nothing to write on, with a few students hitting the double whammy with nothing to write with or on. Yet they all have the newest I-phones.
- Move into the lesson I prepared meticulously the night before, sacrificing time with my lady who never lets me hear the end of it.
- Realise that the students aren't "feeling it today" and are not into it. Quickly move from meticulously planned lesson into uncharted waters of uncertainty and try to create a new lesson on the fly to boost student engagement. Make sure to remain confident as students will riot if they sense I am wavering.
- Consistently answer the questions "Sir, what are we doing?", "When will we ever use this?" and "Why is this important?" on a loop for the next 10 minutes. Do my best not to headbutt the wall.
- Check the time on the clock on the wall. 9:15am, this lesson is turning into a doozy.
- Continue with the following for the remainder of the morning lessons.
- Work with individuals and work with small groups of students. Implement programs for intervention for students at academic risk. Extend students that are academically capable.
- Differentiate lessons to make the most of student learning time. Introduce new activities, online learning tools, and educational games.
- Maintain 25-32 (depending on class and size) independent relationships with students.
- Scale lessons back and make them more structured to help support student learning further.
- Take away scaffolding of lessons as the more able students in the class need to be challenged.

- State lesson objectives, content to be delivered, and lesson expectations. Then continue to repeat these continually on a loop every five to seven minutes.
- Teach students algebra, proportions, and rates.
- Teach students common courtesy and respectful behaviours that will help grow society into a better place.
- Recess time. I am looking forward to coffee. Not getting coffee now, students need me to stay behind and help them with work from the lesson.
- Counsel students. Talk with students about why they are sobbing at their desk quietly with their hood over their head.
- Talk to Student Services about a student's work that has not so pleasant illustrations all over it which has me a little concerned. Spend the rest of the day fighting off concerns that this student may do something to harm themselves.
- Break up a student fight on the way back to the mathematics office. Spend twenty minutes debriefing concerned parties, filling out paperwork, and consulting with school administration team.
- Constantly question myself about whether I am making a positive difference in this world? Remind myself that good things take time. Jimmy Jargon just skated past the office yelling "fu$k the world, I am free!". Him and his period three teacher must have had a heater of a lesson.
- Next period is scheduled planning time, time to get that coffee. Head to the staff room for the first time of the day. Remember to smile and make eye contact with staff members that pass by, but not too much eye contact as I may find myself having to take on extra responsibilities for the third time this week.
- Remind staff as they walk by and ask me why I have not responded to their email that it is not a power move; I have just been trying to change student lives within the classroom during the morning sessions and haven't had a chance to get to them. Please bear with me as I will get to them.
- Abort coffee as there is that "one staff member" hovering around the coffee supply just waiting to talk to someone. Only problem is, it is always a one-way street in that conversation.
- Back in the classroom. Teach Statistics and Probability, confirm to students that yes, we are in math class and no I will not teach you how to count cards (I wish I knew how).
- Reaffirm to students that although learning can be frustrating, that is a good thing, and the struggle is real. Perseverance will be key in life.
- Dodge pen thrown at my head.
- Lunch time. Yes, Coffee at Last! Wait, lunch duty, no time for coffee. Get to my duty area. Conduct initial scans of the area and make sure all is well in my territory. Head over to the student smoke clouds and watch the group try and disband quickly as they see me walking over. Laugh to myself about the 6-foot-4 120kg student trying to hide behind the skinniest tree in the yard, as he does his best to rid himself of his smoking implements. Deal with student.

Teaching: We do it for the money and fame...Volume 2

©

Myles O'Kane

- Pick up rubbish while on yard duty to role model good productive behaviours. Spend fifteen minutes washing my hands as I curse what "good productive behaviours" may have got me into health wise. Duty done.
- Return to the classroom to teach Decimals, Fractions, and Percentages. Students will love this lesson. Students did not love this lesson. I didn't think it would take Fifteen minutes to get Billy B to sit down in his chair. Mind you that is five minutes faster than last week, so it is the little wins, I guess.
- Head to the office to gain some much-needed respite. Colleague X (the difficult one) is whipping up a fresh brew of frustration. I will head to the staff room. Colleague Y has already found her piece of drama for the day. I hope we don't make eye contact. We make eye contact, and she is making her way over here, I act like I care.
- Head back into the classroom to teach Trigonometry. Watch students lose their minds as I mention we will be heading outside again today to measure the length of the shadow cast from the school's flagpole. Remind students it is either this or page 163 from the textbook. Students run out the door.
- Final session of the day, year 9 Dream Team, let's do it! Twenty minutes into the lesson one of the male students in class was giving one of the female students in class a hard time. She walked over and dropped him while I was speaking. Female student is now outside of our classroom doing her best to re-enter the classroom to finish off old mate as she kicks, scratches and screams at the door, I start to ponder.
- Head into the office for the final time for the day in a hope to debrief with colleagues. Colleague X is still going on about woe is me, will call it a day.

As I finally walk out for the day, I see a student sitting on the pavement in the car park waiting for her parents to get her. She reminds me that she very much enjoyed today's morning lesson and she is learning and overcoming difficulties she never thought would be possible. I thank her for her compliment and remind myself as I get in my car, I truly do love what I do.

Things that will Happen First Day of School

The majority of your colleagues will be in high spirits and refreshed after school holidays. Staff that are not usually the positive type will be discussing plans to change students' lives and be the best teacher ever. This will usually last till week 3 of the term, then their inner beast will be summoned.

Introductions and Ice breaker games. Here is where the divide between seasoned staff and not so seasoned staff lies. Usually, the younger members of staff will be all about the ice breakers. Getting to know your class, learning about the new members, etc. The super experienced teachers in the school will start the curriculum day 1 period 1 and remind the students there is nothing like a good worksheet to get to know one another.

Before a teacher even steps into the classroom for the first day there will be a time where a careful study of each individual class list will be conducted. It is usually in the department staff room where cheers and hisses can be heard as each staff members goes through their lists with a fine-tooth comb. "Why is student X back in my class this year!?", "Is student Y's last name the same as student X if so, I hope the family differs from student to student.", "Why are there forty names on my list when my classroom capacity only holds thirty students." These are some of the more common calls I have heard. It is not unusual at this point for staff to start haggling with one another to get an early jump on the student trade season.

The department photocopier will get an absolute flogging the first week back. Reams of class-sets of worksheets will be photocopied, even though perfectly good textbooks lie unused in Teaching: We do it for the money and fame...Volume 2

Myles O'Kane

classrooms. True personality traits will be on show now as staff try new and inventive ways to hustle their way up the photocopier queue to make sure they are the ones to be prioritised. You may find yourself in for treat and the copier will break down mid copy with a breakdown for the ages. You will find yourself following the guided steps only to end up in a whole new realm of technical understanding.

As much as we live in a world where we want all things equal, well at least equal enough so it suits the individual in question at the time, the dividing up of classroom supplies for the school year is always a classic case study in effective teamwork. Textbooks will fly off the shelves only to be found with one teacher having more than others. Calculators are a sticking point for math teachers, especially the ones that are doing all the computations that are needed for high school maths. I have walked through my colleagues' classes over the years to find stashes of calculators hidden in separate spaces or hiding holes. Pencils, erasers, and rulers follow this pattern equally.

You will never be the first one to make it to the duty roster. I have tried and tried again to be in the rare air of the first staff to choose duty areas for the year, but I am still to make it. By the time I get there, there is usually canteen duty and the back oval, which takes half of the break to reach, then I must do a lap around to make sure nothing out of the ordinary is happening before I need to prepare myself and return to class to make sure I make it in time. Find a way to get to the duty roster first and it will make a positive impact on your year.

You will swear off eating from the canteen. I do It every year. Especially as Australian schools start the year on the back of New Year's Eve, I am usually raring to go for the first few weeks of term. The problem is time. We are all busy people and even though every year I tell myself this is the year that I will do it and pack my own lunch each day at school, it seems to fizzle out pretty quick.

Living with a Teacher

We were out at dinner recently with another couple who are teachers. My wife is not a teacher. We started talking about life in general, as you do, with the conversation eventually steering to work. As soon as we got there, we all exclaimed loudly that we were breaking one of the rules of living the teacher life, which is not to talk about school outside of school hours. We laughed, but my wife looked confused, which got me thinking; what is it like to live with a teacher? Are there common patterns to my behaviour? If there are, is it just me? I sat down with my wife and this is what she told me.

She told me that for her the most obvious one is when I lapse into *teacher voice*. If I need to explain something to her, I jump straight into teacher mode making sure to explain everything down to the finest detail. I laughed then explained to her the reason I do this is because I have conditioned myself to put more effort into the first time explaining something so I can avoid the 40-50 times that will come after; "Sir I don't get this" or "Sir this is not making sense." I thought about this a little longer then saw how for me it goes the other way as well. If people are telling a story or trying to explain something to me, I have a habit of keeping them on track. If they start heading off into another direction, I need to keep them on track and make sure they are delivering a straight directive.

"What else, my love?" I enquired. "Well, it is not so much anymore, but there was a time there when you had the need to discipline other people's kids." Again, laughter crept over me as my mind wandered to times I was able to pinpoint this. There was the time my wife and I were out for breakfast. We were enjoying the morning when a couple of kids between the age of 5-7 started playing up on the table next to us, running around, bumping into us. The parents weren't intervening much, and I let it go the first couple of times. By the time the third occurrence rolled around the kids received a stern talking too in my best "you have disappointed your teacher" voice. Then there was the time many years ago I was lined up at a fast-food counter waiting to place my order. There were a bunch of teenagers a few positions Infront of me in the queue being ratbags and giving customers a hard time. Nothing too intense, just a little cheeky. After a while I couldn't help myself and spoke up. Nothing too crazy, just reminding the crew that we have all been young once, let's get it together and work together so we can keep this line moving and get into our food quicker.

"Ok, sure I can see that" I responded. "Anything else?" "Well, what about your collection of whiteboard markers we are acquiring above the fridge." How very true I confirmed in my own mind under my breath. I had just added to this collection the other day completely by mistake, as I walk around with markers in my pockets all day and for whatever reason they don't always make it back to their home at school. I will return them all one day. I swear. My wife went on. "What about the dreams you used to have." "I have no idea what you are talking about." I replied, knowing full well my dreams can be savage at the best of times. Sleep talking and sleep walking are never too far away. My wife started laughing to herself out loud. "When we first started going out and I would stay over you would have all kinds of dreams. I remember one time you started scolding a student, telling him you were going to give him a detention to make up for his lateness and call his parents. The funny thing about it was you were very coherent in your wording, and it felt like I was right there."

I guess there are certain traits that come up when living with a teacher. I imagine it would be the same for most industries. Doing something 40 hours a week is going to find its way into the subconscious at one point. At least the dreams seem to have calmed down now.

That Class

I have always had that one class each year that at one point will push me to my limits. I refer to these students as my *Dangerous Minds* class (after the movie), the students who feel that they are no good and have probably spent most of their school career being told as much. I still find it fascinating how a little patience and the willingness to challenge a student's self-limiting beliefs can lead to some impressive moments.

Standard characteristics of this class are:

- Being cool is the number one priority and education is not cool. These students are extra alert when it comes to sniffing out anything to do with work and will be onto you straight away.
- They will push you and they want to see you crack. As mentioned previously a lot of these students have been told they are no good, will never make it, were hopeless from the start. As a trust building exercise, they want to see how far they can push you and if you will snap. Being patient and remaining positive with these types of classes is the key.
- Their reputations get in the way of their academic progression. Some teachers will mistake these students' lack of work as being not intelligent enough to handle the work, but it is usually the opposite. They can't be seen to be doing the work otherwise what will people be saying in the yard.
- Progress with these types of classes can be incredibly slow to start with. Depending on previous teachers and education experiences they may not be at all excited to complete work. I still find it interesting that students in these classes usually have high resilience in life (most have a sad back story) yet their resilience in education can be low.

How to handle these classes:

- Do everything you can to soften the energy of this class. These students are usually your heavy hitters, students that are constantly sent out of class, get detentions, and more throughout their high school career. If you can start the lessons being calm and relaxed it sets the scene for the remainder of the lesson. Don't get me wrong this requires discipline and will take time. Still to this day if I have a particularly tough class, I will perform the two-to-three-minute ritual of getting myself into the zone for that class. It may be as I am walking to class if I need to switch room from the previous period, or I will shut the door and begin the process if I am already in the class, reminding myself to stay cool, calm, and collected no matter what.
- Me against the world. It is kind of like when the octagon door closes in a mixed martial art fight. The door snaps locked and there are two fighters that are going to go toe to

toe to fight for the win. Now teaching is not as dramatic as this, but it can have that feeling of teacher vs everyone else. Do your best to constantly remind students who is in charge here. No elbows though!

- Focus on the little wins. There have been plenty of times I have walked away from class at the end of a period thinking to myself "Gee-whiz that was a cracker of a lesson." But usually in not so PG-13 language. I just do my best to remind myself all I have accomplished this lesson so far is the students are sitting in their seats and most of them have a writing instrument on their desk. I leave the class at the end of the period 20-30 minutes later to realise that maybe one student has done something. That is your little win to focus on.
- Stay cool, calm, and collected. Bottom line is these students want to try rattle you early. Most of these students have a PHD in disruptive behaviour or at least putting in some serious work to achieve it. Remind yourself whenever possible to remain, cool, calm, and collected and don't let (or at least don't let it show) that these students are getting to you. At the end of the day these students want to do well in class, and they want someone to believe in them, you just must go through their initiation process first to prove it.

There are always tough classes out there. But if my experience is anything to go by, once you win these students over the student-teacher relationships are very productive.

Teaching the Little People

"It is like trying to round up stray kittens" Is how a colleague once explained to me how it felt trying to get the younger years of high school students to stay on task. This saying came shooting to my mind recently when I stepped into a year 7 class for the first time in years to take a relief lesson. These were the main things that came to the forefront of my mind teaching the little people this day.

The obvious one is the physical size difference. The first student that came bounding up to the door to line up for class I had to do a double take asking them if they were indeed a year 7 student that they hadn't just exited the bus at the wrong stop and convinced themselves that everything they once knew about their Primary School had changed overnight. I haven't felt like so much of a giant in my life before as walking around in the classroom that day watching all the little eyes stare up at me.

Their level of constant energy throughout the lesson was impressive. It felt like each student was a wound-up spring waiting to uncoil. Granted the lesson was just after recess and it was towards the end of the week, but it was definitely there. As a teacher you can almost feel the energy transmitting through the walls as you see these personalities come bounding up to class from break. To take this experience to the next level wait for the students to start consuming a gallon and a half of any nearby energy drink. This will surely take your experience to cliff top heights.

Drama, drama, drama. I used to think the explosion of reality TV onto the scene had led to the uptick in drama in the Secondary School yard, now I just believe students are out for the attention. I laughed to myself when during the middle of the lesson one student called out loud "sir she keeps looking at me." Two reasons why: A) In a big person class this may be interpreted as a sign of affection and students at the elder ages all get a little weird trying to process these thoughts. It is a beautiful thing. And B) If the gaze were to go beyond the acceptable amount of time in my experience that statement "Sir she keeps looking at me" can become a whole lot more hostile with less Sir and more what the f##k.

The level of neediness was second to none. "Sir can I sit with my friends?" "No, this is your assigned seat, you can sit here." "Sir can I borrow a pen, pieces of paper, eraser and most of the other items in the stationary box." "You can but surely you have some form of equipment with you." "Sir can I go get a drink?" "You just had recess, plus there is a large water canister on your desk I am sure you can handle it". These are all samples of conversations that were on five-minute loops with various students as soon as they walked into the room.

The Whinge-a-lots

Why reach for your goals through perseverance and overcoming resistance when you can just whine about everything instead. These have been the top performers in terms of student whinges in my time teaching.

"Sir, I don't get it." Usually, this statement comes up just after I have spent fifteen minutes meticulously explaining the concept, demonstrating multiple strategies that students could implement, and explaining everything needed to the last detail. This question normally goes hand in hand with the student that causes you to stop and start your explanation as they were playing around at the back or as you were presenting you could see the students off task and not wanting to listen. I get it, let me teach everyone else as a collective, then I will deliver a special one on one lesson to your good self, as paying attention like everyone else is beneath you.

"You never taught me this." This one is a cracker and usually makes its appearance when students gaze upon the first question of their assessment. They have panic stricken faces as they realise their decisions to avoid doing the work in the previous lessons has now not paid off, but why take accountability for your actions when you can just shift the blame to somewhere else.

"Sir, when will we ever use this". This feels like an ingrained response from every student during most lessons when I first started teaching Maths. As I have become more experienced and am able to link concepts to everyday life more these days students start to see the connection, but it's fair to say, in my initial days it felt like a lot of skill-based questions with not a whole lot of relevance being applied. Mind you I still have days where I leave a classroom and fail to see the importance between the content item just taught and sustained student growth.

"It is too hard" is an automatic response from students when they hit a challenging piece of curriculum. It has been during these times I have had flashes of doing away with the math curriculum then and there to replace it with sessions of "harden the f##k up", but I imagine my presentation to the various stakeholders necessary to fund such an initiative may not be high on their priorities.

"Sir, this is too easy" usually comes from the student who is doing their best to avoid work. However, it all comes undone when you head over to the student's desk and realise that by too easy they just meant nothing is done.

If I go a day without hearing one of the above, it is an anomaly. Doesn't mean I don't shoot silent thanks to the powers that be.

Teaching: We do it for the money and fame...Volume 2
© Myles O'Kane

Myths and Legends

These are the common myths and mistruths I butt my head up against on a regular basis.

Teachers work 9am to 3pm: I have become better at cutting my hours down. When I walked into the industry, I felt like I could barely keep my head above water at the best of times, needing all the hours in the day to keep up with the workload. I was young at the time, with barley any commitments outside of working, so my work managed to fill the void. These days I am militant-like in defence of my time and if I am walking out of school past 4pm it better be a good reason. It took me years to get to this point and this is still requiring me to do a few hours on the weekend to keep on top of things.

Anyone can be a teacher: "How hard can it be, you just get to hang around and play with kids all day." This is what someone once exclaimed to me when I met them for the first time and told them I was a teacher. My first reaction was to punch them in the face but as the anger subsided It made me think of the image of teachers to the non-teaching world. Obviously, this could not be farther from the truth, as most people know. Being an effective teacher requires a boat load of interpersonal skills, content knowledge, with a dash of humour here and there.

All teachers are born with a load of patience. It helps to have patience, but to say all teachers are born with a load of patience is simply untrue. I have met many a teacher that has minimal to no patience. Just because you don't have a desired level of patience doesn't mean that it is not a skill we can learn. Like anything, the more we do it the better we become.

Students always master things the first time you teach them: Being able to reach each student in your classroom and get through to them on some level is what separates good teachers from the rest. Another one of my pet hates is when I must assume the role of a student outside of my teaching life and the people in the teaching role become frustrated if I don't understand their instructions the first time around. Most of the time I dismiss their attitude as being ignorant or inexperienced with the teaching world, but if I am paying for a service and you are failing to get through to me and putting it all on me there is another thing coming.

Finally, those who can't do, teach: This is the biggest blow when someone outside teaching brings this up. Usually, it is off beat or the person trying to be funny, but it gives you a snapshot of how society regards teachers these days. To work in such a place, where every moment is different from the next and filled with so much uncertainty and change. I tip my hat to anyone who has pulled out a whiteboard marker and attempted to teach the future generations.

How Teachers Spend Their Holidays

Holidays. My bone of contention with most people who do not work in the industry is. "How hard can it be, you are never more than five weeks away from holidays." "You get 12 weeks of holidays a year, I would go through all that pain just for that amount of holidays." "You are serious, you get paid for school holidays?" All these quotes have been spilled to me over the years by people who are not teachers. I used to get up in arms, defending my rights to school holidays. Mercifully, these days I just add fuel to the fire and claim the amount of holidays we get is simply not enough. I started to write things down as I was sick of having to defend myself on the spot all the time. At a party one time I met a new person and made the mistake of mentioning I was a teacher, then waited as the person unleashed a three-minute tirade on why teaching and in particular school holidays were a joke. I simply asked for his phone number and sent him what school holidays actually look like for teachers.

For me, the length of holidays determines my character for the set of holidays. The short (2 week) breaks I usually need at least the first week to recover, as I am exhausted from the term. All my adrenaline finally wears off and when my body realises it is not heading to work the next day, I will crash. The longer holidays are usually the same, however; as we break from school the week before Christmas the adrenaline keeps on pumping, managing holiday crowds, shopping, etc. Usually by the end of the holidays I have started planning for the next section of term or the new year hoping to get a jump on the curriculum.

My celebration rituals have definitely changed. Gone are the days of crawling around the city till all hours of the morning looking for the next bit of action or drama to find. I must admit, it was a rather nice feeling after having a large weekend out and walking through the city on a Monday morning, watching all the workers hustle and bustle as they made their way into the office as I slowly made my way home, not to rise from my bed for the next 24 hours. These days, not so much. I still usually head to the end of year staff party but, again, gone are the days of going shot for shot with the local booze hound, trying to establish my reputation as the hardest drinker out there. These days I barely touch the booze. Not for any high moral reason, more that the hangovers are getting too much and wasting too much time. Don't get me wrong, for all my teaching brothers and sisters out there, you do you.

Finally, my ability to socialise has severely decreased as time goes on. During the term I am surrounded by people and people's problems all day. I am constantly navigating the best ways to move forward and trying to predict what the reaction in behaviour will be. By the time holidays roll around I am ready to have a break from people. I need to recharge. Over the years I have become better at managing this. Initially I would hide indoors for a week, barely heading out my front doors. Not so much that I didn't want to or was afraid of running into people, more that I just didn't have the energy at the time. I remember in my early years of teaching I was still playing football. By the time I remerged to head to training it would take me a minute or two to readjust to being around people again. Over time my teammates got used to it and would just ask me "Mylezee! You on holidays again? You are getting a little distant."

Excursions

It is the day the students have been looking forward to. They have done the hard work in class, behaved, attended, persevered, and tried to better themselves academically. At least that is what the perfect picture in the teacher's mind looks like. The reality is, in some cases the student managed to fill out the assigned paperwork and had a parent sign it, so they booked themselves a spot on the bus.

I have been involved in many excursions over the years, here are a few of my experiences:

I took a class of more devious students a reward day excursion out to an outdoor maze one time. The day started well, being that the bus wasn't set on fire on the way to the location, and after a few quick rounds of mini-golf we were off to a flyer. However, when we hit the main attraction (the maze) and split off in our groups, it would only take a few minutes for anarchy to kick in. Students became frustrated with being lost in the maze and unable to find their way out and started climbing the walls to be able to direct one another. Unfortunately, as there were other people other than our school on the course, we were told to exit the venue in a timely fashion, which all students took extremely well. Nothing better than having a forty-five-minute bus drive home trying to figure out how you will tell your principal that you were evicted from the premises.

I was down in the city with a bunch of students from the country one time for an excursion, the reason for which escapes me now. One of the activities for the day was to take the group of ten students to the movies. Easy enough, I thought. Not wanting to cramp the students style I sat off to the side of the bunch of 15–16 year-olds. Halfway through the movie there was an altercation with an adult couple in front. When I made my way over there to help sort out the situation it took a few minutes for the couple to realise I was the teacher and their reaction changed altogether. Still a little surreal playing middleman to a bunch of adolescents and a couple in their mid 40's.

Another teacher and I took a group of sixty students to a water park one time. Being both in our mid 20's at the time, our strategy for supervising the students was a little different back then to what it would be now, with our focus being to lead by example, or going as hard as possible on each activity that came our way. Our first activity for the day was to scale the large Teflon-like tower which reached about 10-15 metres high, with its interior made up of zig zag patterns of seat belts to help support us. Students climbed up and when they reached the top students climbed down, is the briefing we got from the person running the activity. We both climbed to the top at break-neck speed only to have the internal support collapse beneath our weight when we reached the top. Luckily enough it was a medium pace drop to the ground with no real injuries sustained. When we looked at the supervisor, she told us that she forgot to tell us there was a weight limit of 70kg's per person, a limit we both blew out of the water by a solid combined 40kg's.

Laser tag always seems to bring out the best in students. For whatever reasons, I have ended up at various laser tag venues across the state over my years. What always gets me about these days, is the students who are usually well behaved reveal a whole other side when a little competition is in the air.

Being able to work with students outside of the classroom is nice from time to time. However, always remember to be on your toes and keep your head on a swivel, because when it goes south, it takes a sharp turn.

Math People

Ever felt like a complete fish out of water in your life? This was me attending my first ever specific Mathematics Professional Development Day. I remember sitting in a large auditorium with over 1000 math teachers, thinking to myself, *I am in the wrong place*. Being young at the time and having flown down from the country to attend, I remember catching up with friends into the wee hours of the previous night. The keynote speaker threw out a problem and we were to work in pairs. I remember the fear that shot through me as my partner turned to me, an elderly gentleman who seemed like the reinvention of Aristotle as he spoke. When I have told this story to friends over the years, I always have a punchline in there about how in between discussion of strategies, I was biting down on not throwing up on myself, or just by being in my presence that morning my partner became drunk through osmosis. The reality is, I just felt like I was not good enough and didn't belong.

Over the years, I have grown into being a math teacher and am truly proud to be one. Here are a few characteristics and misconceptions of Math people.

We don't all sit around trying to solve sudoku in our spare time. Funnily enough someone asked me this once, if that, indeed, with any spare time that we had we just sat around solving puzzles all day. I had to slowly calibrate my response, stating that although I am sure there are certainly math teachers that sit around and do this, the expectations and responsibilities of any teacher's day see us unlikely to have much spare time at all.

We do want logic and rationale to prevail and we get slightly nervous when we hear non-math people in school settings propose new ideas without fully thinking through the implementation of the process and coming off half-baked. Don't get me wrong it is not a defiance, we just value using our time efficiently and want to make sure everyone else is on the same page. "No need to reinvent the wheel here" was a common phrase I would hear when working with my more seasoned math people back in the day. Knowing me and knowing my tendency early on to go straight to left field, they wanted to make sure they were keeping me and everyone else on the same level from the jump. God bless!

The office dynamic has a few common characteristics among math people too. Most of my experiences will have math people take pride in their organisation skills. Desks will be beautifully subdivided into current tasks needed to complete along with a structured filing system somewhere to make sure any document needed to help put perspective on the past, present, or future, is ready to go at a moment's notice.

Some of the funniest people I have met in my time are math people. Their dry,no thrills approach to putting together a gag had me in stiches many times throughout my career.

Teaching: We do it for the money and fame...Volume 2
©   Myles O'Kane

Math people, you rock!

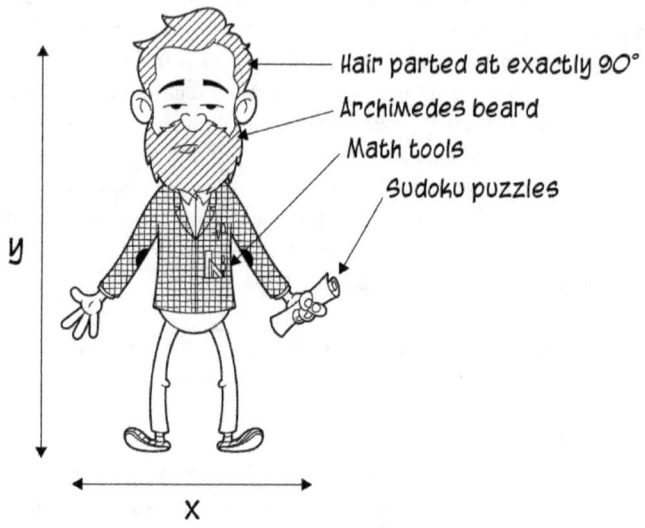

Teaching: We do it for the money and fame...Volume 2
Myles O'Kane

Morning Teas

"We will just look to scale it back a bit." Don't mess up your department's spread, you may never be able to fully recover. Having a set time for people to come together and share some food while they catch up can be a good thing. Whether it is in your departments or staff wide, it is a nice chance to bring everyone together.

I was three years into my teaching career and had just moved to a new school. I had dabbled in a few morning teas here and there while I was doing my time up in the country, but these were whole staff affairs, so I was part of a department contribution with staff that didn't know what I provided. Unless it was something rather decent then I made sure to tell everyone. I was five weeks into my time at a new school and was up next on our weekly internal department morning tea roster. Nothing to worry about here, except the previous two staff members "offerings" were nothing short of impressive, so I knew I was in for it. I remember being up till the wee hours in the morning the night before, slicing fruit in the most intricate of ways, while I made sure the homemade cake was good to go. Two things dawned on me the following day after the morning tea was complete. 1. I was never going to take out the championship belt for best morning tea provided and 2. I was never going to spend this amount of time in preparation ever again.

Over the years, I would start to see a pattern. These days I enjoy being in a new school when the morning tea roster comes out, as I can rely on my seasoned veteran experience and pretty much pick which colleague will bring what food. The young single lads are all about the hot food, usually varying amongst mini pies, sausage rolls, and curry puffs if it gets interesting. There can be a few expectations to the rule here, like the biggest lad on staff rocking up with homemade cupcakes he had made. Not judging, I just appreciate the effort. The more seasoned family men will head more towards a sweet tooth, nothing over the top though. Maybe a few packets of almond fingers, a selection of gourmet dips or possibly a home-made banana loaf, if bread making has recently become a newfound hobby. The ladies in the house always steal the show here. Ranging from a vast selection of colourful fruits to homemade pastries and meat pies. To this day I am still impressed with the level of commitment ladies go to for these get togethers. Finally, the showstopper, usually a staff member from home ec or a staff member looking to make a late run of king or queen of morning teas. I have experienced everything from homemade profiterole or fondue towers to large selections of carvings of meat. All impressive to boot!

Putting on morning tea is a good way to bring the troops together in an informal setting. Just don't be caught short when it is your time to provide, you will never live it down.

Why I Became a Teacher

I always worked with younger people, usually through sports in my younger days; in various coaching positions, captain, senior member in teams, etc. I hated going through high school. I was going through a dark period in a time where still much was unknown and people were not as open about drawing attention to themselves. Progress in school seemed unimportant, when at times getting out of bed in the morning was difficult. I guess I say this as I never thought about becoming a teacher.

I managed to get my act into gear (mostly) by upper High School and received entry into university to study Economics. To this day, I still haven't got much idea why I chose this degree. I guess having taken it at school, it seemed mostly a lot like common sense, something that unlike other things, came naturally to me. Three years later I graduated and wanted nothing to do with the industry, so did not pursue full time employment and took off to travel instead. The idea was to come back to Australia after some time and complete a teaching degree, then use this as my travel ticket to see the world for a few years. I managed to make it back, just never left again, and with 14 years in teaching I am as passionate as ever.

This is why I teach:

Making a difference is number one on the priority list. What does making a difference look like? Having students overcome their self-limitations. Teaching at the schools I have taught at, many students have had a hatred for maths. Working with students to overcome this fear or hatred and see the students grow is a big win for me. But it is not just in maths class. Even though most of my work is done within the maths class, there are many life lessons students can learn. My biggest satisfaction is having students overcome their self-limitations. Having a student persevere a little longer, ask a question in class in front of their peers, or even just come to class consistently are reminders to me of the difference I can make on a day-to-day basis.

Learning things for yourself is not easy and takes time. Although it can be hard at times, I have found by putting myself in difficult situations is how I learned a lot about life. Being a role model for this to students makes me proud to be in the profession every day. If I can offer advice or support somehow to the next generation, I am all for it. It feels good to be able to learn from mistakes. Maybe in a perfect world making new mistakes would be sufficient but luckily enough we do not live in that world. Being able to pick a student up, push a student when they want to give up, or support a student when they feel unwanted are all powerful things to do.

Finally for generations, even centuries previous, teaching was respected as an influential position in society. Since I have been in teaching, it has almost become a backup plan for many teachers, along with lower entry requirements into university and teacher courses. I guess in some way I want to help restore teaching to the once respected profession it was.

For all these reasons above I would take teaching over a high salaried job any day of the week.

Has Time Changed Me?

Coming from a long line of teachers I was confident when I first started. Not cocky but confident that I had enough skills to keep me "alive" to start with and I would grow over time. Looking back now, I wish I had kept a journal of some sort as a record of my thoughts when I started teaching compared to now. It would be interesting to see if the deeper philosophies still line up or the path has taken me somewhere else.

A while back my uncle from Ireland was over visiting us in Australia. At the time he was retired and had been for a while, an ex-primary-schoolteacher for 20 years before he moved into another field later in his career. He told me teaching was a young person's game. At the time I was still relatively fresh to teaching so didn't think much about it. Now it makes me think. I am a decent way into my career and in my mid 30's at the time of writing this. I stated teaching when I was 23 years old and felt like I was bullet proof from losing energy and exhaustion, not from making mistakes. These days I must make sure I am matching the task that needs to be done with the time of the day otherwise my energy stores will be all off, making life that much harder.

My philosophy of being a teacher is still the same, that we as teachers play an important role in society and have a responsibility to help guide the future generations. This was a lot more simply put when I first started out, "changing lives" was all that was needed to sum it all up. I am more understanding these days, at least I think I am. When I first started and would see the experienced teacher who was grumpy and bitter, I would vow to myself that I would never turn out like that. These days I am not excusing it or saying it is the correct attitude to go about life, but I understand life changes over time and anyone who has been in the teaching game for a bit can see this.

I have mentioned previously, when I first started out I was militant in the classroom, especially with behaviour management. It frustrated me to see students so disorganised and slack in terms of work ethic. It felt like I was a drill sergeant getting my platoon ready to run over the trenches. These days I am still big on these things but approach them slightly different. Instead of fighting every battle head on, I try to be more patient these days: barely raising my voice, reminding myself in these moments that not every lesson can be a life changer.

Finally, the big one, technology. Even in the last 5 years technology has evolved faster than my previous 10 years before that. When I first came into the industry, it was all about preparing students for 21st century learning and how we can integrate technology into lessons to make students more comfortable and prepare them for the workplace beyond school. These days it is about confiscating phones in class and making sure students who have been involved in indiscretions online are kept apart in class and the yard, all the while fighting societies ever-decreasing attention span and ever-increasing addiction for screen time.

Some things have changed, and some things have stayed the same. I guess if you can be honest with yourself as a practitioner and understand your strengths and weaknesses as an educator, we will be able to focus more on growth and continue to raise the tide for all boats.

Enter the Bull Pit

Whole school staff meetings can be a mixed affair ranging from school to school. Some schools I have worked at, staff meetings have been very polite and considerate, most staff being respectful of one another. I have heard stories, but have not verified these stories, of some schools' meetings where staff members talk over one another, have their backs turned and even are quite disrespectful when anyone from the leadership team gets up. I have been at schools where the whole school staff meetings are a good social affair for people to come together or a chance to catch up where business would not normally permit. One of my favourite ones was when a neighbouring schools' principal was delivering a program, I can't remember the specifics, they tried to capture the attention of fellow staff members by saying "ok 3-2-1 and listening". We had never met her before, and we certainly did not appreciate being treated like students.

The whole school meeting gives you a good indication of what the school looks like in a moment of time, where morale is at, and has a culture been developed. Are departments sitting together, or is it more free range? Are staff generally respectful to the information being presented, or is there constant push back on most of the information being presented? Is information just being presented so people involved can say they have ticked that box and move onto the next box? Is it the same people presenting, or are different staff stepping up and taking on responsibility? In my mind a healthy staff meeting should be open to discussion and constructive feedback should be taken on by all if needed. Ideas should be presented but presenting possible solutions is equally as important. Then, as a whole staff, we navigate the best options for our journey as possible. Not to say that this will not be without setbacks and failures, but we learn together.

In saying that, the most fun thing about attending whole staff meetings for me is observing the types of characters that appear. The "popular crew" will have a section to themselves with a lot of banter going back and forth. This group can sometimes get up to no good playing word bingo and other such games. The eager-to-impress colleagues usually don't take long to find their feet during a whole staff meeting, finding any way to interject to tell everyone that "In my class we are doing this", as if they are the master in the room and have it all figured out, everyone should bow down to their greatness. Then there is the colleague who is all words and never any actions. This colleague announces twenty different possible solutions to any problems that arise, and I admit this colleague has had me a few times nodding my head in agreement to their suggestions. The only downfall of this colleague is that they are never anywhere to be seen when the time is needed to implement any of their suggestions. Finally, the wise veteran. This colleague has been around for a while and a bit in the teaching game and has seen it all. Why make any changes without consulting them first? They have seen it all is the usual line they will give you.

Even in meetings that have reminded me of the wild west at times I have been reassured that as humans we all just want to be heard and appreciated, and if we can keep that process to a rational efficient manner, it may just go a step in the right direction of helping society grow to a better place.

Parents Attack

At times teaching can feel like you are being smashed from every direction. You have a rough day in class with the students playing up, it feels like you are fighting constant battles in the classroom. You may then have someone in admin breathing down your neck over something which adds that little more spice to the day. Finally, you return to the office to take a two-minute breather and you find you have a parent's number scrawled across your desk, and they are waiting for your imminent reply.

What I am still a little bamboozled about is parents' reactions at times. I remember one time I gave students results back after an assessment. This student had just recently been moved into my class and was a little out of their depth. I returned to my desk the next morning to find a mini thesis email claiming all sorts of things from this parent, a reaction that was over the top. A quick phone call and explanation of the situation saw the parents do a complete 180 with their attitude and they began thanking me for my suggestions for improvement moving forward. Another time, I was at a parent night early on in my career with a notorious parent who loved to "shred" teachers apart any time they thought an injustice against their child had occurred. She was basically a bully who enjoyed making teachers sweat. Possibly her payback for the way teachers treated her when she went through school. Who knows. I could see she was locked and loaded when she reached me. I taught her son in year 8 maths. To be honest he was not a bad student, just had a lot of energy. I started in my usual way. Anytime she started to mount an attack I reminded myself to stay calm and remain firm but fair. By the end of the 10-minute block she was nothing but positive. Now at this point of my career, I have seen it all. Parents coming down to settle scores with students who may or may not have been picking on their child. Parents coming down to settle scores with staff they think may have done them or their child wrong. There is always a common approach to dealing with these situations effectively.

Always remain calm and seem in control. I know it seems basic and some people are better doing this then others, but it is a skill set and like anything the more you do it the better you will become. Don't respond to emails in the moment. There have been plenty of times I have read an email from a parent and seen red, telling myself "Surely you know your child. Do you think this went down exactly like this?" Most times these days I respond by phone. It is good to be able to put a voice to what the situation is and talk through the situation and ways to move forward. In any meeting, whether it is face to face, over the phone, etc, always remain respectful to the parent. Just because their child told them their version of the events, doesn't mean there is not some truth in there. Be open to change to help rectify the situation. Finally, don't be defensive. Both parties want the best for the child/student. Find the problem, but more importantly spend more time on how to work towards progression.

Like I said before, it is a skill. The more you do it, the better you will become. It just takes time, hang on in there.

Being a Role Model

Teach the curriculum, foster effective learning practices, and support individuals to become better students were my main goals when I started teaching. I barely thought beyond a lesson, let alone the classroom, and certainly did not consider myself a role model at 23 years old.

Sure, teaching curriculum, building rapport, and encouraging students are all important facets of a teacher's life, but I think some of the strongest impact you can have on students is leading by example. Actions, not words. Showing the future generations how to be decent and hopefully help society grow into a better place. Now not everyone who signs up to teaching considers themselves a role model, just like every professional sportsman sees their first job as getting on the field and playing to the best of their ability and takes whatever comes after that, after that. But if we can have more positive role models in the world, surely this will take society to a better place?

This is what I consider a good role model in a school setting should look like:

Actions not words: This is probably the biggest stand out feature to me. Anyone can tell someone to do something, people do it all the time. But to do what you say you are to do is the way. As the great rapper DMX (RIP) stated, "walk a mile in my shoes, then know why I do dirt on the street."

Be human, make mistakes and learn from them: I had a football coach once that told me "Don't be afraid to make mistakes, just don't make the same mistake twice." Now I was only 15 years old at the time, so I was destined to continue to make mistakes over and over again but being confident to try new things and make mistakes is important for growth. I still see it in the classroom these days. Students are afraid to contribute as they worry if they are wrong the judgement from their peers will only prove that they are in fact not that bright, removing themselves from future participation. I make mistakes a fair bit in class. I always make sure to thank the student for correcting me and showing that I am unfazed and ready to move forward.

Manners: When I was in primary school my friends' parents used to constantly try to correct me when I called them by their last names, Mr and Mrs such and such, instead of their first names. I was young at the time so never thought much about it, but it was a sign of respect. You are my elder, you get this title. Manners go a long way in a tough class as well. Most of these students are trying to protect their reputation as tough and disrespectful so will initially confuse kindness with weakness. I am not saying you should bend over backwards for students but demonstrating good manners will help turn the environment of the classroom into a better place.

Set the standard: It is all well and good to throw out high expectations in a class, but if the students don't see the same standard from the teacher they will feel hard done by and start to rebel. If you need your students to work, demonstrate that you are working as well. Hit the whiteboard session hard, make your way around to small groups and actively get involved. Even the simple act of tidying up the classroom while students are in it drops the little hints all the time that we are all in this together.

Mistakes Made

You need to make mistakes to grow. I am a big believer in this, and students need to see other people making mistakes to feel comfortable themselves to make mistakes and learn.

Over the years I have given students plenty of times to take comfort in my ability to make mistakes. Here are some of my better ones.

Misspelling every word under the sun: I jest here. At least a little bit. But my spelling is far from impressive. Recently I was completing an assignment on student truancy rates. I had my notes on the board, it was lunch time so I needed to have them up quickly. It wasn't until a student came into my room and asked, "Sir, how do you spell truancy?" I didn't realise he was being dead serious. I replied, "I am pretty sure it is the way on the board". He replied "You have spelt it four different ways.", which I had.

Leaving my iPad out: I had a particular rat bag year 9 class one year. This day I had to leave my classroom and run to the office quickly. I had been teaching using my iPad, which I thought I had disconnected. When I returned a few minutes later there was a massive photo of me posing on a beach (which I had taken for a lady I was seeing at the time) projected onto the screen.

Using sport as an incentive with an intense year 7 class: This class is the hardest class I have ever had. A bottom year 7 class with only 15 students in there, but they truly were on another wavelength. Earlier on in the year I had the bright spark to mention to the students that if they behave well, I will take them down to the back oval to kick around a few balls. The moment I let them run loose from the classroom I knew it was going to be a disaster, as they purposely ran through two structured sport lessons which were taking place at the time, then managed to lay into each other once they had arrived. By the time I arrived students were in tears, yelling at each other and cursing each other out. It is this moment I knew that we would no longer be visiting the sporting fields as an incentive in maths. To hammer the nail home the sport teachers whose games we ran through put in a formal complaint against us and from this day till the remainder of the year we were confined to our classroom.

I slept in a ditch: In the last week of my final prac in the country we threw a house party to commemorate our time. It turned out to be a decent time with plenty of booze being consumed. At one point after countless shots of tequila I managed to separate myself from the party. The rest I don't remember. My housemate found me later that night sleeping in a ditch with a bunch of students standing around. Lucky nothing came of it. He managed to walk me home that night and get me inside the house. I headed to school the following Monday thinking that I would have to resign as a teacher. But not a word was spoken about it by students. By staff it was a whole other story.

Leaving a student behind: We had just returned from a whole-day school excursion. The vibe was good stepping off the bus, until I realised my number of students exiting the bus was short. This was in the day before mobile phones had become a thing, so I jumped in my car and made the 30-minute drive back to the venue. Luckily enough, I found the student quick. When I asked him how he missed the bus he simply replied, "I wasn't ready to head back to school yet."

Survival Tips for Graduates

Congratulations you have graduated now let's see if you can survive.

I have mentioned it a few times already but when I was growing up teaching was the farthest thing from my mind. I was a rat bag at school and did not have an interest, at least back then, to stand in a classroom and deliver a monotonous lesson, something that I had witnessed for most of my schooling life.

At one point, something changed. I saw the profession less as delivering curriculum and more about helping people. What can I say? I am a sucker for helping people. I did wish I had a record written down somewhere to look back in my initial years of teaching, something written down by a person that has had experience and is willing to talk about their successes and failures. Maybe this is it, or maybe this is just someone writing words down on a page, but these were things that helped me when I was fresh out.

You have to want it. Sounds like a sporting cliché, and maybe it is, but to be good at anything you have to be passionate about it. There will be days that you walk to your car at the end of the day and mumble under your breath "what just happened", knowing that you are in a profession that does good by people, can help you keep it together.

Be disciplined in keeping everything. I spent copious amounts of hours initially in my career reinventing the wheel. Creating more resources, assessments, feedback sheets, etc., all because I had not kept original documents. This can be a serious "smack your head against the wall moment" especially if it has kept you up into the early hours of the morning and now you need to reproduce something for your period 1 class. Although most of the world has transitioned away from physical copies, it does not hurt to have a mix of both hard and digital copies.

Keeping yourself emotionally balanced throughout the short term is the key to survival early on. The profession is too demanding and requires you to give too much of yourself to get caught up in the small details, and trust me, there will be plenty of times and incidents that occur that you want to react to. Starting each day fresh and without judgement from previous days sets you up for the mindset of growth and progress. Keep yourself and students accountable, but don't let previous days emotions get in the way of present or future decision making.

The first two years you are in teaching are the hardest. The workload feels like it is never ending, the profession itself has ever increasing expectations and there's times you feel like you are devoting your life to this career. Don't. What I mean is, set strict time boundaries for yourself. There were plenty of times I was in the country, and I would be walking out of school at 5 pm. Now I was young and didn't have a family to worry about, but there is a real chance that the initial years of this job will eat at you. Set strict time boundaries and remind yourself that even if you are the most effective worker under the sun, there will always be more tasks to complete.

Gifts from Students

I remember talking to a colleague one morning. He was telling me how his partner is a primary school teacher and at the end of the year she cleans up with presents. He stated out loud, "It must be a beautiful thing." before we did a quick compare and contrast of situations, reminiscing on a present a student had left my colleague earlier in the year, a lovely message scrawled across his classroom exterior wall in spray paint exclaiming "F*ckyou Mr *, you remind me of this." With a large sketched penis taking up the remainder of the wall.

As much as I compare with other teachers and whinge about being hard done by at times, it is not all bad. Actually, far from. These are some of the better gifts I have received over the years.

Endless coffee supply: I am a caffeine addict, or at least I was. I have cut back a fair bit now. Only two cups a day. Takeaway from a café on the way into school in the morning, along with an instant cup just before lunch. This wasn't always the case though. One school I worked at ran a certified hospitality course and had an industry sized kitchen that the students would operate out of on school grounds. On certain days, students would deliver coffees to different teachers (mainly admin). I managed to get myself on the circuit, however, there seemed to be a misunderstanding as I would receive my coffee halfway through the period, then another student would come down with another coffee towards the end of the period. The longer I was at the school and got to know the students, the more the caffeine intake increased. It was a lovely thing. I would be teaching at the board and there would be a knock on my door and a student would appear with coffee in hand and sometimes food they had made. Only problem was by this time in the day I had usually had 3 students make coffee. As I did not want to be rude, I had to find new and inventive ways to disappear the student made goods.

Hand carved goods: To this day I still have some of my past students' handywork displayed in my house. I remember at one school; I must have been in the middle of moving house and the students somehow found out. At the end of the year, three of my students presented me with their hand crafter goods: a chopping board, outdoor table, and a wooden chess board. They told me that they "understand teachers aren't on the best money these days so hopefully these gifts will help you with your set up." I was touched.

Christmas cards and student notes: It is easy to remember just the bad at times. To think about how we are hard done by and how unjust the system is. I tried from early on in my career to keep any notes students pass onto me. There have been plenty of times in the past where I have gone to this box of student musings and managed to muster enough strength to head into class for the following day.

As much as I can become frustrated that at times, I feel my hard work goes unsung, I catch myself and remind myself that sometimes the reward is just knowing you have done the hard work or gone the hard yards and tried to put society in a better place.

Bamboozled

A decade and a half in now and although nowhere near as frequent as they used to be I still have more than enough tough days. Usually on these days as I walk to my car at the end of the day I think to myself "Am I doing this right?"

Bamboozled is the feeling I get when it feels like I have just been hit from every different direction. I am doing my best just to survive the day, dealing with my stuff personally, doing my best to support my colleagues around me, when out of nowhere seventy-four different things come flying at me from all different directions. Getting control of your emotions is key not just in the classroom but dealing with staff as well. Here are some tips to get your emotions under control.

- Make note of where your emotions are at before you even step out of the car into the staff car park first thing in the morning: Mornings that I am feeling sluggish, or tired, stressed. I make note of this. I give myself a little more leeway for the day.
- Remain cool, calm, and collected: This sounds a lot easier than it is, but like anything, I believe it is a discipline and can be trained. There have been times in the past where I have seen red with a student and lost it. These days, unless it is super warranted, a disapproving look or a simple correction of attitude is what I look for.
- Communication: Anything that involves relationships, clear communication is the key. Students understand better when they are being asked to do something rather than just told. Sure, the student should be able to figure out that repeatedly pressing the on/off button on the computer is not going to speed it up, more like decrease its hardware, but letting the students know what and why can save you a little heartache.
- Take time for yourself: It used to be the teachers huddled around the tree next to the tin shed at the back of school grounds, sneaking a smoke before the siren sounded to end break time. These days tea and coffee takes its place. Even if it is only 5-10 minutes, make yourself a cup, or even walk to another kettle in the school to give yourself time to calibrate and refocus.
- Prioritise your tasks for the day: This has been a massive saving grace for me. In a profession where your time can be hijacked, I have found it is important to have key tasks that I need to complete for the day. There are always going to be more tasks, but if I can tick off the most important tasks for the day, I am satisfied when I am finishing up that day.
- Stick to a work schedule: Again, this took time for me. Being able to keep work within the hours of 7:30 am and 4:00 pm has very much helped my mental health in recent years. I just remind myself that I am not responding to emails, and I try to limit planning as well, outside of these hours.

All in all, there are still days that pop up and put me through an emotional carnage, but by following the above I feel more prepared and ready to take it head on.

My Best Hacks for Teacher Time-Management/ Productivity

Learning to protect my time has been one of the hardest but most important strategies I have had to work on as a teacher. As teachers are generally helpful and caring people, taking on more to help others almost becomes second nature at time. Before we know it, we have taken on more and more and we are now drowning, feeling overwhelmed, and a little bitter, that the industry is making us do more and more. It is not so much a flat out no, or blanket no, to every request more just that I am not bending over backwards for people who are not responding in turn. This is still a learning process for me. I find, especially, that when I start at a new school I want to be seen as a good team player and before I know it, I have taken on a heap of tasks with a large portion of these tasks being outside of my area of need.

Planning my weeks and days ahead of time has made a real difference for me. Each week I plan out my list of tasks that need to be complete for the upcoming week. From there I prioritise that list to make sure the top of the list is my "must do" tasks and I put my "hopefully" tasks towards the bottom. Any tasks that I do not complete I then roll over to the following week. If a task has been on the list for a few weeks and is not getting done, it may be because it is too wishful thinking to be able to get to it or the task is not important enough to complete. From my weekly list I select three-four big ticket items each day that I need to complete. I schedule these tasks into my calendar and completing these tasks is my mission. For me, my daily calendar is sacred, and anything that goes on the calendar needs to be completed.

There is a difference between helping people, so a rising tide lifts all boats and bending over backwards for people who are trying to offload and handball you more responsibility. Learning to say no to people is an important skill and although it may sound easy, it takes a little work to get used too. These days I am fine with it and rather enjoy telling people who I sense are trying to get one over on me that no, I am going to sit this one out. However, if I am stuck, a nice little technique I have developed (passed onto me by one of my seniors one time) is to tell the person I will think about it and get back to them, which saves me having to answer on that occasion, especially if I can't figure out the right words then and there. Again, if it is a staff member who I know would do the same for me, or barely asks a favour, I will go above and beyond for that person. However, sometimes it is a case of once bitten twice shy, when I meet people for the first time and they take advantage of my good nature. Ok, that is fine, you got me, but that has set the tone for our relationship down the track.

Assigning the right task to the right time of day has been a nice little focus for me now. Knowing myself and knowing where my energy is at throughout the day becomes highly relevant to what tasks I assign myself during the day. I know that in the morning when I first arrive to school my critical thinking is the best. This is when I attempt to complete any tasks that require the most amount of thinking. Towards the end of the school day usually my mind is mush. I am tired and my energy is starting to wean, making life a little more difficult. Replying to emails and planning my lessons usually seems to fall into these time categories. Working in time intervals, as swell, has proven successful recently. Working for no longer then 50 minutes on a task followed by a 15-minute break helps recharge my energy and get me in the right mind frame to continue.

Finally, consistency is a big one for me. Working in the environment of teaching means that there is a large amount of unknown from day to day. Set times for arriving and leaving school has worked wanders and always reminding myself I will never be able to get everything done, helps ease the pressure of high expectations we place on ourselves in and outside of the classroom.

Teachers Going the Way of the Dodo

"You have Google, search it up." To which a student replied, "Sir, does that mean Google has now replaced teachers?" I laughed at the story my colleague had told me in the staffroom one morning, but deep down I worried there may be some truth to it.

One thing that the constant evolution of artificial intelligence has done is speed up the efficiency of industry. When self-service checkouts replaced employees at supermarkets, I thought "no worries", it was a job that seemed to make sense to become automated. There was no way the robots would take over the world. Then when I was working in the country next to one of the biggest mine sites in the Southern Hemisphere, I overheard a conversation one night where one Fly in Fly Out (FIFO) employee was explaining to another FIFO employee that their job may be heading the way of the dodo, as mining companies were looking to introduce remote activated machinery, meaning that physical human capital would no longer be needed on site as much of the machinery would now be controlled by an operator in an air conditioned room somewhere in the city. These evolutions in industry had me thinking, even slightly worried, surely teachers could not be replaced by artificial intelligence?

Before I jump in with my future predictions, let's consider what the industry could look like in years to come. The year is 2040, students now head to school, but it looks a little different from the usual. Students head straight to a computer room somewhere, where their morning mathematics lesson is about to begin. At first there are only students in the room; quiet and in their own world, with their headphones on, before an adult appears from around the corner and announces, "good morning class, please prepare your screens as your lesson is about to begin." Now there are different ways to go from here. Maybe students have different differentiated programs that take them through their own set of problems designed specifically for their ability level, or maybe there is a mass broadcast from a big screen in the room which all students are plugged into and the content is being delivered by some kind of robot somewhere in our world.

Aside from schools needing frequent access to more than one or two computer rooms, let me tell you why I think this wouldn't work. Imagine a rowdy year 9 class heading into the computer rooms after lunch. The big screen lights up and all you hear is "Get fuc#ed, there is no way I am letting robot-sir teach me again, I get so bored." Although the ability to differentiate could be greater if controlled solely through A.I. The personal skills and behaviour management skills will still be needed, granted that all A.I. hasn't become more charismatic and charming than your average teacher by this time or schooling hasn't been thrown into chaos and there are security robots able to physically remove students from misbehaving.

Myles O'Kane

One possible situation, I think, that may possibly occur is a merging of human resources with non-human resources. Where artificial technology delivers content to the students and teachers would be reduced to more of a support capacity, working with individual students or small groups of students, depending on the students.

Let's just hope it doesn't become any more than this, as it would be horrific to see the human element taken out of the teaching profession.

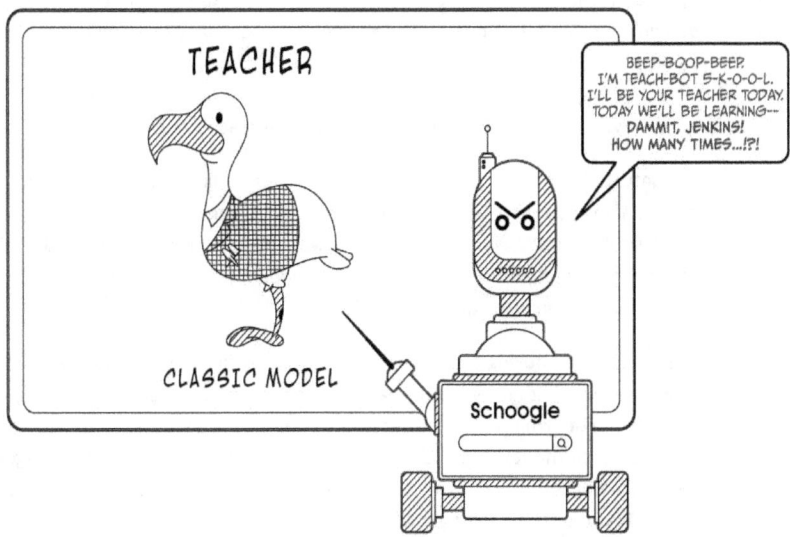

The Sanctity

Computer rooms. These rooms can feel like a sacred space in public education. You have physically seen the room; you know there are computers in there, yet every time you jump online to try to book a room, they seem to be booked out 13 months in advance.

21st century learning, these days, means being able to access technology is important. Most, if not every subject, has reports, assignments, or investigations that students need to complete, so having access to technology becomes of the utmost importance. Booking students into a computer lab for a lesson a week can be considered a must, however, there are different ways to handle these sessions. Don't be the teacher that has the student's login while you sit back and read the paper. Nothing would frustrate me more than having missed out on booking the computers only to find the teacher that snapped up my spot is just using it for free time.

This is my observations of these rooms so far in my time teaching:

- Etiquette of how far to book in advance: In the early days of my career, I would book out the same day every week for the term. I had to make sure you got in there as early as possible, basically as soon as the roster went up and you would be fighting off other teachers left right and centre. These days I book maybe 3-4 weeks in advance, then renew as I go. Keeps me under the radar.

- Misreading the booking sheet: These rooms can be fiercely contested at times. From reactions provoked, it feels like teachers have laid down their life to gain entrance. Reading the booking sheet incorrectly or, even worse, just rocking up and hoping for the best, is on the fast road to making you no friends amongst your colleagues. The look on a teachers face as they walk through the door with 30 year 8's trailing them only to find the scheduled class already in there working away is priceless. On the flip side, there has been a time or two where I have misread the booking sheet only to realise that I'm in the wrong place, the feeling in the stomach is far from priceless.

- Have respect for the space: It is a blessing to have several rooms of computers all up and working, but too many times teachers are just sitting back at their desk while Billy B is over in the far corner destroying every remnant of hardware, slowly taking down the future usage of the computer lab one letter of the keyboard at a time. Think about your fellow colleagues, maybe they would like a session with less time on their feet and more interactive student learning. You keep this up, everything starts falling apart. Be respectful and get it done.

Let me tell you how I would do it

Getting told how to do anything by anyone with minimal to no experience in what you are trying to do, usually sets off a series of red flags for me. Most of these statements (I don't ask their opinions on the matter) come from people I don't know all that well and most of them have never set foot in the classroom. These seem to be the common talking points that come up during these red flag circuses.

The lessons they would implement: It is funny what you remind yourself of when it has minimal or no reference points to work with. Non-teaching folk love to tell me how they would run the class and make all their students super smart. Recently I had a gentleman tell me; "You should just teach them (students) up to their 30 times tables and give them a calculator and teach them how to measure shit." Granted, he was a tradesperson himself, but up to 30 times tables seemed a little extensive.

Misuse of title: I wanted to say abuse of power, but it seemed a little extreme. If this non-teaching folk was a teacher in a class, no student would play up as they (at least in their mind) are a force to be reckoned with. Usually their behaviour management strategies include, holding students back, roasting students in front of their peers, hell even risking their job through possible physical violence. End of the day, until you have stood in front of a class on your own with 30 students staring back at you, that can split off into drama at any moment, to me, that makes your opinion redundant. A strategy I used to go with in these situations, is making a very clear over-generalized view of what the non-teaching folk did themselves for work. It was 50% strike rate; 50% got my point and would filter our conversation into something else, the other 50% would double down and come back with something else they didn't like about teaching. Only two moves remain here. Choke the person out or get your way out of the conversation.

Strike frustration: This one occurs a little less since the pandemic has kicked in and suddenly parents have been stuck at home more with their children, but there was a while where most teaching folk would have a version of "between holidays and strikes do you guys ever get any work done." When a person would try to nudge me as if our relationship has been around so long that I should understand that he is joking and not just a D-head. Again, spelling out the reasons why teachers strike with a description of the teaching climate at any given time was my initial approach, but I got sick of this over time, so now I just let the person get it out as I have one of the songs from *Grease* playing in my head, the one with the ladies saying "tell me more, tell me more", I forget the name.

These above characters are not bad people, just a little limited in understanding the world of teaching. As the great street rapper DMX (RIP) said, "Walk in my shoes and hurt your feet then know why I do dirt in the street."

Types of Teachers in a School Setting

Every profession has its range of characters. These are some of the characters I have crossed paths with, in my time teaching.

Bright eyed and bushy tailed: This character is usually assigned to the new graduate in the teaching ranks: someone who is full of promise, ambition, and heartfelt goodness, which are all great things by the way. They just lack the experience of time in the industry and have yet to come to the realization that unfortunately the cold hard truths of the teaching game will knock them to the floor, and they will need to know how to handle this. Common characteristics of this character include the need to smile and tell you everything in their life is fine and dandy when you ask. They are overly positive (at times they go overboard) about teaching when other teachers are in earshot. Don't get me wrong, it is important schools embrace these colleagues, they just need to be reminded at times that the teaching game existed long before they got here, and they won't necessarily get everything when they first start. Continual support and reassurance will help get the most out of these characters as well.

The tyrant: This character is usually in a position of leadership within a school and loves/needs to use a public gathering of their colleagues to reinforce their insecurity and prove that they are in a position of power in some way. They love to micromanage their employees and any suggestion of not agreeing with their point of views can result in an endless loop of "why they are right". This character is not afraid of conflict, which can be good in a school setting when things need to get done, however, it's usually their way or the highway, which can alienate a large proportion of the school's population. My suggestions for dealing with this character are to remain effective at your job, that way when this person comes waltzing around, you have a strong body of work to fall back on. Try to avoid unnecessary fights but stay strong when you feel your views and opinions are being mishandled.

Hollywood: This character views themself as the most popular teacher in the school, which is to not be confused with the most effective teacher in the school. A key characteristic for this character is that they go by a nickname which they will tell you the students came up with, but I have a feeling they planted it into the students' minds subtly somehow. They are usually in casual dress as this is seen as keeping it real by the students. Finally, this character normally drives a nice car and makes it part of their daily routine to arrive moments before the first bell is to sound and to park in a place where all the students can see them. Use this character as a journal of knowledge when you need to find out more about a student and make sure to have them close by in a potentially chaotic situation as their trust with students can usually settle down an escalating situation faster than most.

The weak link: I was trying to find a nicer way to put this, but I can't. This employee gets away with doing as little as possible as most colleagues tiptoe around their inability and get stuck shouldering their responsibility. This character is not to be confused with someone who is under-skilled but willing to work on their improvement, this colleague instead has a way to outsource the blame to everyone else, rarely taking any responsibility for their actions. It is important to keep this employee accountable. Keep them accountable to the small issues so when big issues arrive it is not a last-minute drama. Also, always stay professional with this employee. This character has made a career of being difficult to avoid taking any responsibility. Keep them on point with short term goals.

The seasoned veteran: This character has been in the teaching game for so long they have become institutionalised in the system. Their anxiety around new things, at times, can be misinterpreted as a fear of the unknown, which it might possibly be, either that or they have seen so many half-baked ideas that they are unwilling to commit until they see further proof of reasons for doing something or at least measures of success. Not usually known for their outgoing manner it will take a while, or some exercises in trust, for them to open up, demonstrated by their need to only take up a position next to other seasoned vets in the staff room. To get the most out of this employee give them a level of respect to operate outside of the group and trust them to deliver results. Specific deadlines and expectations have this character giving a decent level of performance.

Things that will Happen on the Last Day of Year

I can set my watch to it these days. Doesn't matter how the year has turned out, or how I think the year has turned out, these things happen like clockwork.

The first pattern is with the students. Students you have not seen for a time will stroll through the gates on the last week of the year to be part of class again. This is usually accompanied by the questions at one point during the week "Sir, am I going to pass Maths this Year?" to which my only response is, "It is good to see you back in class, I imagine having missed the previous four months of school has affected your overall performance in this class a little." Then comes the students' demands during the last week. They get on these early, some as early as halfway through the term. "Sir, I will not be doing any work in the last week of school." My immediate response is "You are hardly doing any work now, I can't imagine the shift between gears will be all that dramatic". Instead, I smile and let the students know that we will cross that bridge when we get there. Students will riot if you don't offer up a movie for the last week of school. I don't personally go down the movie track, as finding a movie that fits all the students' preferences and the departments guidelines is proving harder and harder these days. Besides, I like doing things a little differently to everyone else and I have bullet proofed my argument against me showing movies to students in the last week.

The next pattern in the universe is the behaviour of your colleagues. The big one for me is those colleagues that have hunkered down over the previous few weeks in reporting, marking, or just want to be out of plain sight, will now start to re-emerge from the darkness and make their way back into the fold. That colleague you have that has moaned and whinged for the majority of the year has now found a new lease on life, knowing it is not long now until they are sitting poolside with a drink in hand. The chatter of antics of the staff party will start to circulate the school during this time. The young bucks on staff have probably already started drinking to make sure they are staff party fit, while others may see it as a chance to disappear into the holidays without a goodbye. One thing is for sure, by at least halfway through the staff party some drama will have kicked off and it is usually between the colleagues you least expect.

Finally, there is the pattern in yourself. You have made it through another year and take a moment to take it all in, the good and the bad. Those difficult students you managed to get through to, the students that came to class a few times but never seemed to make it back. Those lessons which took you to the brink of madness, but you managed to pull it back and continue on. The colleague who you wanted to throttle but you managed to stop yourself as you realised they were just overwhelmed themselves and felt like they were drowning. Someone from the administration team will approach you with all these supposed great ideas that all benefit the school in the coming year. You fight the urge to tell them to get f'ed and let them know that you will reassess the ideas when you start again the following year. You will have fought back moments of insecurity, self-doubt, and fleeting madness. You remind yourself you are in an important position in society as you walk out to the staff carpark for the last time, take a deep breath, and remind yourself you will do it all again the following year.

Word to the Wise

I do appreciate a wise word. Whether it be before I am about to head into a situation for the first time and don't know what to expect or I am heading to the canteen and someone for some reason decides then and there to impart with their hard-earned knowledge, I find myself coming back to these insightful words to help steer me further down my path.

Teaching is all about relationships: This was a recent piece of advice given to me by a principal. I did not think about it much at the time but then it started to sink in. Being in the people business, how you treat other people is crucial. Doesn't mean we have to bend over backwards and let people take advantage of us or go to the other extent and become a tyrant, but it is important how we treat one another.

No one wants to be left behind: Talking to a recently retired Head of Department about how to get staff members in the team to buy in. He simply stated, "no one wants to be left behind." Now that's not to say go off on a tangent somewhere and propose an overhaul to the system for no apparent reason, but if you truly believe in something and have a little proof to see it working, leading by example and commending staff members in small/modest ways can lead to a change in staff thinking.

Start every day fresh: This piece of advice was given to me by a seasoned veteran when I was putting in the hours in the country after school. We would get talking at various points of the day, the most common time being just after school. We would debrief quickly, and I would usually talk about some recent incident that had happened during the day that had me all caught up. The advice was simple, no matter what happened the day before give each student a chance to start again and they will appreciate it.

I never made my teammates do anything I wouldn't do: I can't exactly say Michael Jordan was my teaching role model, but these words ring true. Whenever I need to work with students, staff, admin, I try not to give my point of view if I have not walked in their shoes at least a little. It is all too easy to sit back from a place of comfort and be difficult, it is a different story if you are leading by example.

Whenever you leave your class bring a pen with you: I thought this was a passing joke at the time. The colleague who passed on this little gem to me was in his 40th year of teaching and still a high-quality teacher. I asked him one day what his trick was for avoiding "handballs" from other people when outside of the classroom. He simply looked at me and said "carry a pen and make sure people can see it. They will think you are busy that way."

Living in the Moment

Teaching can provide some of the more amusing situations in life. Sometimes you just must sit back and appreciate the moment.

I had a tough year 11 class once. They were a talkative bunch and barely any work would be complete unless I was constantly on them, and it took my everything to make sure they maintained focused for the time I was trying to explicitly explain the concept. I remember we were a few months in, and the students were starting to warm to me. I tried to be tricky and ended up explaining the concept at the time with too much depth, which I thought would be greatly received with a possible standing ovation as I brought my analysis to a close. Instead, it was received by my students with blanks stares. I could see that my explanation had gone over their heads, so in that moment I decided to go back to the start and re-explain it all. Frustrated that I now would have to break the student's attention to erase my mistakes, then start over to find a better entry point for my explanation, my moment of frustration was broken when I heard one of my students in the front row speak to her peers next to her and state "I hate it when you have days like this. The other day I was trying to spell out school and I couldn't figure out where the H goes. Does it go at the start?" It was here I choked back laughter and reminded myself from little things big things grow.

There was a year 7 student having a particularly tough day. He was bouncing off the walls left, right, and centre. I managed to finally have him settle down and I couldn't believe my luck when he went quiet for a good five-minutes, hammering away on his MacBook, the rest of the class falling quiet as he did so. Little did I know he was prepping the room for his final act. Out of the blue a robotic voice repeated sentences such as "God damn I am f#cking bored" and "Holy shit, maths is the stupidest fu#king thing ever." When I looked over to the student and could see him playing with his MacBook, he simply replied "You *told me* not to talk."

To this day I have not come across two bigger year 8 students than when I taught student X and student Y. Both from Polynesia, they were tall and wide and certainly knew how to occupy space in the room. Both being jokers of the class, I had them sitting in the front row next to one another. I remember one day I sat in bewilderment as I watched these two students try to solve a common classroom problem. Student X had managed to get his backpack back strap caught under the leg of Student Y's chair and instead of trying to solve the problem by simply asking Student Y to move his chair so the backpack could be freed student X went on a verbal tirade against Student Y, blaming him for everything under the sun. I finally intervened as I saw this heading into a cycle of insanity and showed them that all he had to do was lift his chair and his bag would be free.

Finally, during multicultural week one year students were partaking in a range of cultural activities during break. I had a year 9 class straight after and as the siren went to signal the

Myles O'Kane

end of break students made their way to class in dribs and drabs. Throughout the period I could see one of my students looking down at a sticker he had collected trying to mouth the correct pronunciation of the word. Finally, he broke and shouted out "Sir, what does Key-aoi mean?" I had to quickly remove the smile from my face and correct the student that it was ciao, an Italian expression for hello, and made sure to stress the importance of travel and understanding the world when possible.

Sometimes when I am in these moments, I just need to remind myself to live in the moment and take it for everything it is worth.

The Final Countdown

"Sir are we on computers?" This is a common cry from students as they come piling through the door for the final period of the day. Eagerness, excitement to learn, and willingness to cooperate are all virtues which seem to take a back seat for students in the final period of the day.

One of the first things I noticed when I started teaching was the difference in student personality as the day went on. During the morning periods they are still waking up, one or two of their homeboys may not be in class and the litre of red bull they consumed ten minutes prior stepping into class hasn't taken effect yet. The previous borderline angelic student period 1 has now turned into the monster in period 5. Getting the students to settle after lunch is always interesting. These days I laugh to myself when I walk past a teacher battling outside his or her classroom door to have the students get in line. I laugh only to myself as I know the pain and heartache these lessons cause. "Sir can I finish this in class?" Is another common catch cry from students as they rock up to your class with a 1kg box of lasagne bought from the school canteen two minutes before the bell is about to go.

Here are my tips for surviving the final period of the day with an "interesting" class.

- *Bring down the energy of the room:* There is a couple of ways to do this. One of my favourites still to this day is to just start talking to signal the lesson has begun. Now as much as I would love to believe that as soon as the first sound leaves my mouth students shut up shop, pull their posture in, and are nothing but attentive to my every word. This first 5 minutes is a battle. Remind yourself that you are in charge and that anytime a student tries to speak over you just to stop, wait for them to recalibrate their focus, then get back to where they are. Have something structured ready to go. In maths, mental math/lesson starter activities are really good during this time. Anything that encourages students to transition into a time, even if it is brief, of working by themselves. The last few years of my career I have come to appreciate the power of colouring. Keeping it subject based and relatively simple to start so students can have some success will set you up for success in those first few minutes.

- *Use of computers:* Booking a computer room can be a safe option. Most subjects these days have online programs that can be used to help support differentiation amongst student ability. Just make sure you are one of the 'good ones' and keep an eye on your students and don't let them run free a trash the place.

- *Have your rewards built in:* Have game-based activities or even reward type activities, like taking the students out to play sport in the final 20 minutes of the lesson. The first section of work keeps students accountable; the final 20 minutes will keep you sane.

Do what you can during this time, good people. Every time is a learning experience, and you can modify as you go.

Patience is the Virtue

Years ago, if someone was asked to describe me, "a patient man" is something that probably would not have come out straight away. It may have not come out all. I wouldn't say I am not patient, but it is something I have had to work on to improve over the years.

Patience can take several forms in a school. The big one is remaining patient (or cool, calm, and collected) any time there is an attempted coup/power struggle or a situation arises. But it is also important with the smaller things as well. A student is late to class by thirty minutes and when I ask them where they have been they respond I was in the gym and didn't hear the bell. Sure, I want to lose my mind and rain down fire and damnation but, knowing the student, asking him to sit cross legged on the ground outside of the classroom is a slight win and wins are nice.

Teaching in a high school puts the student and the teacher in the same place together in a pivotal moment in the student's life. They are starting to try on different personalities and are trying to see what fits. They want to test their defiance game and high schools are the perfect stomping ground for this. So sure, remaining patient is important for establishing a positive working environment, but more importantly you are teaching students how to react and become productive members of society, which must be the big win!

Finally, patience should not be confused with weakness. If done correctly and consistently, patience can become one of your strongest tools in class. Students understand that you are in control of yourself and the classroom and will start to respect you as an authority figure. To get there though, there is going to be a point where friction is present but grinding through this in the classroom and remaining patient and consistent opens the door to many beautiful learning experiences down the road.

Teaching in Today's Environment

iPhones, social media, streaming channels and online gaming, We have now entered the realm of the business for attention and it feels like I am losing this battle in the classroom.

This generation has been immersed in technology since early years. The need for constant stimulation is crazy and the price paid for a constant feed of information is addiction. When I first started in the profession, if I brought some showmanship to a lesson, with a little humour here and there, I could keep students on task. These days, if I am not performing a hybrid act combining stand-up comedy with a Broadway spectacle students will lose interest and then erupt into chaos. Teachers are quick to blame students for having their phones out or for the constant need for them to be checking the latest updates, but I think we are at times forgetting how strong the algorithm has become now at keeping attention, this is not just a f#ck you to the teacher. Maybe five years ago now is when this first hit home for me. A student kept ignoring me when asking for their phone to be put away. Eventually I made my way over and asked for the phone to be handed to me. The reaction was terrifying, and I didn't really understand what the issue was at the time. As the years have progressed and my screen time has increased, I now understand this addiction. Unfortunately trying to spice up trigonometry doesn't quite compare to the world students created on their gaming console a few nights previously.

I was at a workshop recently. The focus of the workshop was resilience and the presenter started with "You guys are currently in the weakest period of existence." I had to choke down my laughter as I thought back to one of my students earlier in the morning who had broken down when I had to move them away from their friend for the period, as they were being a constant disruption. Students hit a bump in the road now, or things don't go exactly to plan, everything falls apart and it all comes out. Just because they have been born into a comfortable place in the timeline of history doesn't mean we can't teach them skills to better react when situations arise that are out of their comfort zone. Students just need to be taught that they will fail but that is ok, there is plenty to learn from that. To get up, dust themselves off, and go again.

The trade-off with having such great technology at our fingertips is the growing concern for mental health issues. The hours upon hours spent holed up in a room somewhere with nothing but their console is not the best form of living for students. The common response for students back in the day when I asked them what they would be doing for the holidays that were fast approaching was "Eat, sleep, and go to the movie's, sir." Now it seems like reminding students to take a break from their gaming marathons and step outside into the sunshine or try to speak to someone else is becoming more of the norm.

Teaching: We do it for the money and fame...Volume 2

©   Myles O'Kane

The Power Struggle

The death zone, zone of importance, the place you don't want to be. Whatever you want to call it ending up in the power struggle is something you want to avoid often, but if you do end up there you want to be prepared.

Adolescents want to test the boundaries and see how far they can push it. All the time they are gauging your response and updating the data in their minds. Too easy and the floodgates will open early and too hard there will be constant friction and outbursts that will devalue the working environment.

I have had many power struggles in my classrooms, especially early on in my career. From students' blatant refusal of instructions, defiance, and the occasional "F#ck you, sir." In front of the class, these times will happen, and it is important to hold your nerve. In saying that, these are some of the techniques I have found useful when dealing with the power struggle.

Stay cool, calm, and professional: Students want to get a rise out of you. By remaining cool, calm, and professional with the student you are taking any personal conflicts out of the equation. I remind myself to picture the calmest person I know (usually happens to be a character from a fast paced, action packed tv show I have watched in the past) and consciously remind myself to calm down. You will find remaining calm will help you think clearer and act more appropriately in the situation.

Be consistent and follow through: Students want consistency. They will never tell you that but even James Dean, being the rebel he was, needed boundaries to rebel against. Anytime you enter a power standoff make sure you are clear about your process in your head and make sure you follow through. Most of the time it is going to require extra paperwork and follow up, but the student will see that you are not messing around and either will start to operate within the rules of the class or will enter into higher disciplinary measures.

Give the student a way out: Most power struggles are a reaction from something occurring in the moment. Reminding students they have options and are in control of the potential consequences can go a long way in helping remove the me vs you vibe.

Kill the situation with kindness: A student's reputation can mean everything to them at this age. Especially if they identify as being a tough kid in the school if they back down in a situation their reputation may take a hiding, hurting their social standing in the school. Not that a student's social status should be any concern to you, especially when a student is continuing to be disruptive, but knowing this helps my strategy. If I reach a power struggle with these types of students, I make sure that I start and end every direction with please and thank you. These students want to dig in so they don't lose face. With modelling good manners, it takes the macho out of the situation and helps defuse any emotion in the situation to help students think more clearly.

It is not the be all and end all if you end up in a power struggle situation and often you will end up here when you start out teaching. Just make sure you are equipped for the situation and every time you go through it, it will become easier to manage.

Winning Students Over

It is a good feeling being able to walk into a class and feel the warm energy from students as they are ready and eager to learn. Unfortunately, it takes time to set up this environment and it can feel like a grind at the beginning.

A phrase that has stuck with me over my time in teaching is "If a student likes you, they will learn from you." Now I am not saying your objective should be to befriend the students, quite the opposite. Remaining professional, being approachable, and showing that you care goes a long way towards setting a strong foundation for good working relationships. I have found it fascinating to see how it has played out over the years. I have had detailed conversations with maths-content wizards who think that the students will find it incredible to have access to such knowledge in the classroom, yet when I walk past their rooms engagement does not seem to be at its fullest. Students need to be able to trust you. If they don't, they are not going to work for you.

Building rapport with students, in my eyes, is still the most important thing to do in teaching. Strong rapport illustrates a level of trust that, once achieved, allows learning to skyrocket. Here are a few of the strategies I have used over the years to help build rapport with students and win them over.

Students need to see what they can and cannot get away with, early on. Especially with a new class, or if you are new to the school. Set these boundaries early and make sure you are consistent on holding the students to them. The statement "don't smile till Easter", still holds today as much as it did when I started in the profession. Being willing to fight the small battles in the first few months of the school year, and remaining firm but fair, will set strong foundations which you will be able to fall back on if and when times get hard down the track.

Students respect routine and structure. It gives them boundaries to operate in and an understanding of what needs to be achieved. In my career I have only crossed paths with a few students that have totally rebelled against the system. When students start to witness consistency, they learn to trust. They understand who you are. They have enough unpredictability in their life, they need something to get them through.

Stay cool, calm, and collected at all times. Again, this is a skill and will take time and discipline to develop, but once achieved it is a game changer. Especially in those tough classes, students will do what they can to test you and even try to break you initially. Staying calm shows them that you are here, and you will be staying here. Now we need to learn how to work together to move forward.

Teaching: We do it for the money and fame... Volume 2

©

Myles O'Kane

It can feel like you are drowning at times. I get it, you have all these expectations: curriculum, school, your personal expectations as a teacher. You are trying to balance them all, and at times walking out of the classroom door at the end of the period it feels like you have accomplished little to nothing. Look for the small things. The number of times where I have had to dig deep to find something positive to focus on is countless. Congratulating students for bringing a pen to school can be momentous, depending on how you build it. At the same time though, when that same pen isn't brought to class, there is all hell to pay.

Some students will do all they can to buck the system, but deep down most students crave discipline. Keeping students accountable needs to be balanced with noticing the positive changes. Student shows up to class late for no reason, they need to make up this time, student doesn't complete enough work in class, student needs to complete this work. Keep it realistic though. If a student previously barely ever completes work, don't expect the student to move heaven and earth. Just enough to head in the right direction.

One of my favourite acts these days is to meet students at the door with a firm positive attitude. "Good morning such and such", (always use every student's name as they walk through the door) sets the tone for the lesson. It also has the added bonus of spinning students out a little, especially when the class is first thing in the morning and they are still waking up.

The Mouth

I wasn't always like this. I remember when I was young I always considered manners the top priority, to the point that even at sleepovers in primary school when I became familiar with parents I would always refer to them by their last names, even when they insisted first names was more than appropriate. Even now when I am teaching, I see manners as extremely important and do my best to model these things.

In my adolescent's however attitude kicked in and manners seemed to take a back seat. At least for the time anyway. I guess somewhere along the way I developed a problem with authority. If I felt unjustly done by (which was most of the time back then as in my mind I was the ambassador for all things fair and just in the world) and a teacher went in on me, there would be hell to pay. I wasn't afraid to voice my concerns and if the teacher didn't have a clear vision in their head where they wanted to take the argument they would be found out pretty quick. I remember several times a teacher trying to make an example out of me in front of the class. Looking back now, maybe he was wrong and maybe he was right, but at the time I had a one-track mind, and it was me against the world.

Although I am willing to own up to the fact that some of the time I was in the wrong, those times where I felt I was in the right I became a wrecking ball. I was in year 11, there was a new young sports-teacher at the school (early 20's) and he was a divide and conquer kind of guy. We were playing volleyball one time in class and what started as a cruisy game, became a fiercely contested battle when the teacher mentioned I was all talk in an exchange at the net, just loud enough so I would be the only one that could hear it. From there, it was on, and the game ended being cut short by another sports teacher walking by who could see us getting into it. The feud went on for some time. The teacher ended up leaving the school, making sure to add into the yearbook for that year that my newly broken record for the 400m at the athletics carnival the year before, was weak, and was not worthy of being in the books.

Going through this has made me be able to relate better to students. When I have a disobedient student and am working with them one on one, most of the time they just want to be heard. If someone is willing to listen to them and see a little compromise the growth gained in the long term is worth it.

In-school Suspension

Wagging, fighting, and being an all-round nuisance were the name of the game when I was a young lad in school. Year 9 proved to be a standout year for me starting to come into my own and buck the system. The only problem was the system had been around for a while and did not like to be disobeyed.

Back in the late 90's there were differences in the disciplinary system to what there is now. If you misbehaved in class, there was lunch time detention. Although it was rather odd, as you were supposed to report to a central room with all the other students from different classes who had been misbehaving, so depending on the teacher for supervision more times than not it became a free for all of the students. Completing "Scab duty" was doing yard duty, usually your teacher issued you a slip during your class for misbehaving, you were then to take that to the supervising teacher at recess or lunch and once you had picked up your allocated quota of rubbish or after an allotted amount of time the teacher would sign off on your slip and you were free to leave. For the more heavy-duty offences there were suspensions. Days at home with your parent/s may have benefits. Finally, in between all of this was in-school suspension. You were technically suspended but would be serving your time in an isolated space on school campus. In my time teaching now, it seems like schools have done away with this, at least the isolating part, focusing more on restorative justice, which is a good thing. I think.

For my school the location of the in-school suspension was the back of the 1950's stage area. I can still remember it quite well There were eight to ten cubicles set up with big wooden doors that would be drawn closed so only a little light would be able to make its way through. At the start of school, you were to report to the stage area. This would be a holding area where you would meet the other patrons that you would be sharing the stage with. I spent a fair bit of year 9 in this system so I got to know it well. You wanted to see at least one other face in the morning area, a little bit intense for a 13–14 year-old to be spending a whole day by themselves without anyone else, just a rotation of teachers through. Once attendance was taken, the teacher for the morning session would escort you to your cubicle. You were told that you were not allowed anything except your thoughts and your line of vision. There were plenty of times a few hours in when I was craving for something to do, anything, even schoolwork, but it was never going to avail. As my visits increased in this place, I started to become more prepared. Smuggling in this and that, at one point I was becoming gutsier as time went on. My biggest haul was five to six different items including a discman, pack of cards, finger skateboard, and a few other things. All which were confiscated by the various teachers over time.

I look back now and understand why the system was put into place. To break students. To make the experience anything but desirable to try to decrease negative and unwanted behaviour. I imagine today's students having to do this and I am glad they don't have to. Mind you, it would be interesting to see the overall impact on behaviour patterns if they were to go down this path.

Tips for Starting at a New School

For me the worst thing about this process is not knowing. Especially if I have had some time in advance and know I will be moving on or starting new, I must do my best to restrain myself *from* trying to plan for every possible event that could possibly occur in the future and heading into the zone of paralysis by analysis.

Here are a few things I have gathered in my time moving from school to school.

Sit back and survey the landscape. I know you probably want to run in and be eager to impress, I know I was, but if experience has taught me anything, it is best to sit back and evaluate the environment before you start making any moves. This isn't to say be a hermit, don't talk to anyone, and lock yourself in your classroom and office, just be aware that you are the new person, schools can get incredibly tribal so people will be looking at your everything. Don't be afraid to make mistakes during this time. A lot of people want to fit and conform to the social structure that already exists. I guess I have always been lucky like that, knowing that I am comfortable in my own skin. This isn't to say I just rock around the day with just my own company, but I am not desperate to conform, so this gives me a little breathing space. On the other side it can be a little lonely to start with but, again, in my experience going in and setting boundaries early will set you up for the long run.

Every school is different, boy is this true. I have been at schools where new staff (usually people in leadership) have come in and started to tear everything down and immediately turned staff offside. Not saying this can't be done, but if you do, please don't keep throwing the line out "back in my last school this worked etc." Schools may look the same on paper, demographics, economics, and population size but the inner workings of the school may be entirely different.

Get to know the school you're in. Anytime I change school I get to walking the corridors and the school grounds a lot during recess and lunch time. If you start to see what the students are like outside of class, this can help you modify your planning to adjust to this.

It is going to be lonely to start with. I have said before teaching is ultra-tribal at times. New faces won't be accepted fully until trust is built. Take your time. Remind yourself that nothing will be built overnight and that every second in the day is a chance to move forward in whatever you want to do.

Get organised. Learn to prioritize quick. Any time I start at a new school the initial few weeks can feel like a bombardment of tasks. One thing that has helped during these times has been to up my planning game. I looked online and came across several detailed planners through amazon. The one I finally settled on taught me how to prioritize. Any new task that would come to me throughout the week, I write it down and add it to a generic word document at the end of the day. Sunday evening, I look through my list and prioritise what tasks need to be completed. Then each morning that week, usually just before I hit the road, I would spend 10-15 minutes using the planner to plan my day. Now this may seem a little extreme for some people and for others not enough, it is all relevant to personal experience. Get a process to handle your tasks because when you head into the silly season in schools and the tasks are piling up, it is good to have a structure in place to keep the overwhelm at bay.

Have fun and spread positivity. It is easy to get caught up in what is not working. I know I have done it numerous times. However, even finding the smallest spark of happiness can help make your day that much better.

Graduation Ceremonies

These evenings are always quite good, seeing the students take their final steps in secondary education before they are off into the big world. However, like any big occasion, at times they can get a little overwhelming. Here are a few tips to help make the event run as smoothly as possible.

Presentations. If you are involved in any presentations make sure you know your names and how to pronounce them correctly. If not, ask the expert staff member in the field and if you still can't get it ask the student without having to reveal what you need to know it for. Nothing more disheartening for a student who has worked their backside off all year to not be respected enough to have their name announced properly.

Strategize talking to students and parents. Like a parent night when you have to see a decent number of parents, your time will be limited. Have a template in your head of how to talk to approaching parents with their students. I go with a quick introduction and congratulations to the student for getting this far. I then ask the student what their next step is and try to throw in a funny story or something quirky. I then wish the family best of luck and head on my way.

Attitude. Usually this event is for teachers to volunteer to attend and help some of the staff in attendance who want to be there. But if you do wind up at one of these under gun point, do your best to remain positive. This will be the last time you will probably see this group of students and you want to make it as memorable for them as possible.

Staff members and their territories. Some staff members or a particular staff member may have been assigned to the organization of this event since the start of the year. They see the success of the event as a reflection on them, and so they should as they have put a bucket load of work into the event. Unfortunately, however, the not-so-positives start to arise as well. Watch the control freaks in the staff rise out of the woodwork on this night. For some reason totally sane staff members turn insane, for at least moments of the night and it is usually the ones you don't expect. Giveaways that this is occurring are when they walk around like they are super important, making sure to be seen by everyone to be delegating tasks and will even try to get you to repeat their instructions out loud once they have finished telling you. This usually starts the night off in the right way for me. I once had to position a ladder at a ceremony so the photographer could climb up it to take the final photo of all the graduating students. I had six different people try to tell me six different ways to carry out this task. Relax, people and trust in your colleagues.

Crowd control. Now this has been a very rare thing in my time and only recently had to take on this role. We had a graduation for our students in year 11 with engagement issues and unfortunately one student realised he would not be graduating mid ceremony so he kept repeatedly yelling out "Dog c''t!" to the staff as they were presenting, nothing was done until a parent of another student had to walk over and tell the student to be quiet, but in a more working class you-better-understand-what-I-am-saying way. Have a few staff members present who are good with behaviour.

Exams

They have been on the books all semester. Students knew they were coming but for some reason still considered them a mythical thing, even up to the week before they are due to be sat.

Exams are an important part of school assessment. Especially in upper school, working towards the final exam, any preparation students can have in the year or years previous will no doubt be beneficial towards them. As it stands now, the final mathematics exam in Western Australia is worth 50%. Students hear that number and start to panic; other students hear that number and figure one quarter of their final mark distributed from the exam doesn't sound too bad. I guess in these cases not knowing the math has its upsides.

These are the patterns I have witnessed, particularly with upper school students, when exam time comes knocking.

Most students think they are the exception to the rule and a single "cram" session before the exam will suffice. I know I certainly thought this way when I was a student. I remember studying for one of my final exams, I had a mate over and any time we threatened to focus and do a little revision or study we usually lasted a small number of minutes before we were out on the basketball court outside, justifying to ourselves that we deserve this break and there was no need to worry as the four pack of red bull and an all-nighter was all we would need to get by. This proved not to be the case. I have my students chip away at the process of study from early on in the year. Teaching students to study is important, having the students develop the discipline of study themselves is the most beneficial. Implementing two to three 45-minute study sessions, four times a week, has the students in good routine when exam time comes rolling around. Going the extra step and detailing to students what they should be studying each session has proved useful, no point staring at a blank wall for 45 minutes at a time.

On the day of the exam there are two extremes. "Sir, I can't wait for this, I am going to crush it", or "Sir, is calling in a bomb threat to the school still a thing?" Seeing students right before the exam is always interesting. If I am setting up the exam, I usually get to the exam room early to make sure everything is there. As the exam ticks closer the waiting area starts to fill with students and the conversations will begin. I remember heading into my last exam when I was in school. I told myself I would get there early, sit away from friends, and use the last minutes to do final revision. That lasted about three minutes. By the time I arrived on the scene seclusion and study were the furthest things from my mind. I remember specifically trying to sit away from my group of mates in this class, only to have two of them sit one in front and one behind as soon as we got into the room. These days I do my best to stay in the exam room until it is time to let students in. I used to head around and do my best to make students at ease during my early days, however, these days, I greet the students at the door and for any student that has entered panic lock down I do my best to reassure them that it will all be over soon.

The instructions have been read out; students are all locked in this room together for the next few hours, now it is time to get through it. One of my favourite parts of being in the examination room is watching students' expressions during reading time. From when they open the front page some students' fleeting confidence is decimated as they progress further into the questions and realise they are out of their depth. On the flip side, the look of joy that spreads across a student's face as they realise that their hard work is now paying off is not so a bad thing. This extends into later parts of the exam too. Periodically, I will look up from my desk to see a student staring at the ceiling, I imagine they just promised themselves that this brain-break is what they needed, however, it seems to have taken over.

Teaching the Top Class

These are your top students, the students which will be leading society into its next dawn, the students that will be looking after me and probably you. These are my go to's when teaching the top Mathematics classes.

Unlike the more challenging behaviour in some classes, which want to test your will to survive, these students want to see if you have what it takes academically. Again, they have been identified as the brightest, so they believe they have every right to challenge what you have. There are a few key techniques which you can fall back on to win the students over.

Hit them with some big maths early on. When I say big maths, get the large equations up there, have questions which sprawl the whiteboard so when students come in, they see your work and hopefully start to question themselves and their attitude. Just make sure you know the solutions, as this may prove to be a little embarrassing if you fall through at the final hour trying to prove it all.

Be comfortable making mistakes. These students are waiting for you to make a mistake so they can find it out and then announce it to class in a statement that says "look at me, I just proved the head maths person wrong in the class, obviously I am destined for greatness." Don't let them fluster you. Acknowledge your mistakes and calmly remind yourself that the best mathematicians are not necessarily the most maths gifted, they just learnt to embrace the struggle and grow from their mistakes. Then take a mental note to get the students back, down the road.

Lesson differentiation. Lesson differentiation is important for all students. These students require it a little more. Try to find activities that twig their interest or ha them thinking outside of the box. If they have this brain power, let's put it to use and try to sculpt the future minds. Instead of just throwing the more "challenging" questions from the textbook at them.

Remain confident. These students can sense you wavering and as soon as you do they will jump in. Have students teach a concept to explain their process and working. Suddenly the most boisterous students seem to go missing and quiet down as order is restored.

Like any class, once you can build the right environment for this type of class lessons will usually become a rich learning experience and keep you on your toes.

The Lost Art of the Whiteboard

In this day of digital technology, the use of the whiteboard has become less prevalent. Blended learning, 21st century learning, flipped learning, educational research is always looking for the best ways to incorporate technology into the classroom, and so it should. However, what happened to all those whiteboard ninjas out there who could piece up a board with skill and grace.

Below are my criteria for outlining what it takes to be worth your weight in gold in whiteboard prowess.

Letter formation and angles. To this day still a large thorn in my side. My cursive was never very good. This was evident by being the last one in my primary school class to receive my running-writing license and although the following year I moved up the rankings to be the second-last person to receive my pen writing licence, it was fair to say greatness in penmanship was never on the cards. I am better these days, still far from great, but most of my letters and words maintain the same spacing and direction when on the board, so although I keep it brief on there, it is improving. If you want to be considered in the elite in whiteboard usage in the teaching game, your writing on the whiteboard needs to be exemplary. Letter formation, spacing, and tidiness are the three check points here. A tip of my hat to my primary school colleagues out there. Some of your boards that I have happened to stumble across are very impressive and should be the standard across the state.

Spacing and order. Your spatial awareness is always going to be on show, especially being a maths teacher, so whiteboard spacing is going to be crucial. No point clustering all your need-to-know information all over the board, synced order and flow is of the utmost importance. A few years back I had just finished putting my notes up on the whiteboard for a year 11 ATAR class that I was running after lunch. I was more than a little happy with my effort, making sure to praise myself on my deliberate and dedicated effort to have all my letters and words running in the same direction. When I opened my classroom door to return to the outside world a colleague just happened to be walking past and see my notes up on the board and the smile across my face and mentioned "not bad." He went on to say that he still felt fear shoot through him every time he remembered back to school and the notes he had to copy down. Fourteen boards in one maths lesson was his record. Granted, he was near retirement so it was a different time back then, but it goes to show the change in the profession. If I have my students put their name at the top of the page and spell it correctly that is considerable improvement for the week.

Colour coordination. Mastering the whiteboard really came to the forefront of my mind working at a school recently. One Friday morning, 4 gents (including myself) all over the height of 6 foot 2, were down in their rooms side-by-side preparing their whiteboards for some serious period 1 action. It was only when I was darting in and out of the different rooms to

Teaching: We do it for the money and fame   Volume ?

Myles O'Kane

gather resources for my lesson that I realised the incredible whiteboard skills each of these "big men" possessed. Not only was everything lined up perfectly with adequate spacing and logical order but the use of colour for headlines and to demonstrate key points was second to none. Fair to say as I dragged my feet back to my classroom in disillusionment, I decided then and there I could no longer lean back on the view that being a big man myself excused me from adequate whiteboard skills.

Students Cheating

I can't figure out whether the future generations coming through schools these days have become less intelligent or just lazier. This is never more apparent than when catching students in the act of cheating during class assessments.

These are some of the better ones I have come across:

Overly suspicious movements within the bag. Any time a student's hand dives down into their bag during an assessment my eyes follow them down. Usually, I can see the panic in the student's eyes as they try to stall in their bag. When I ask them why they are taking such a long time, they are looking for their ruler, even though I have provided them with one on their desk and they have never brought a ruler to class in our time together. The same goes for suspicious movements in a pencil case. Just recently I had a year 7 student that had some notes stashed in his pencil case during an assessment. The student's consistent gaze and focus on the interior of his pencil case gave it away, that and the fact that I had never seen this student use a pencil case before, so it became particularly peculiar when he was suddenly fascinated with the contents during the day of our assessment.

With today's technology, students using phones during assessments must be a no. I know it sounds straightforward, but students will find any way to get you to let them use their phone. The usual one in maths is "Sir, I will use it as a calculator." One school I worked at, a teacher fell for the trap, unfortunately, and the student managed to ace the assessment piece. Why this was of particular interest was that the student had done little to no work for most of the semester, yet when it came to the assessment the student achieved a near perfect mark. It was investigated and found out the student had an app on their phone which could solve any equations you place under the camera. Being that the whole assessment was on algebraic expressions, the student had struck gold.

Students trying to sneak a look at notes during their toilet break during exams. This was more of an old school one, but it still happens. The student will have something written down on a piece of paper somewhere or scrawled across their arm, covered up by a jumper or long sleeve shirt. Common signs here are that the students will have little to nothing written down before heading to the toilet yet when they return suddenly are full bottle on all the world's knowledge. Well at least they think they are.

You can sense a student's confidence level when early in the assessment their eyes start to wander. Adequate spacing amongst students in a classroom sitting an assessment is a necessity of course, however, at times the right amount of spacing is not always available. The ability for students to cast their gaze far and wide across the classroom for any piece of information which may help them has never ceased to amaze me, even better when the teacher and student's eyes meet halfway and suddenly the panic kicks in following the question "how long has sir been looking at me for?"

Professional Development

It is part of the job. If we want to get better at our jobs or stay relevant with the research out there, we need to continue to upskill ourselves in the profession. For years I hated this process. I was young and overconfident and thought I knew it all. It is only since I have mellowed a little in my recent years that I have started to unlock the true worth of professional development. Mind you, I still have PD's where it feels like all I am being told to do is to suck eggs.

Here are a few patterns I have witnessed emerge over the years:

The presenter. Having an external presenter or someone from outside of the school can break both ways. The presenter is a new force and an unknown identity to the school. No baggage is attached. However, being teachers and knowing the difficulty of holding someone's attention if you don't capture it straight away, this can be a problem. I have sat through death-by-power-point so many times in my career that I think I can almost predict the structure of the presentation before it even starts and if I must do another jig-saw activity on butcher paper after a full day of teaching I swear the fire for the revolution will be coming.

Level of involvement. I am a big believer in "actions not words" and for that reason I am not the most overly active person these days, however, there are certain colleague personalities that like to become extra involved during these days. *The junkyard dog.* This is the colleague who sees any opportunity to throw a little doubt into the situation, anything that will give them a chance to put their argument skills on display. *Look at me I know it all.* I can't think of a better way to sum up this personality, but I am sure you all know the colleague. Any piece of research that is presented, or any new strategy that is trying to be implemented, they have been there and done that and they need to be seen as the most important. *The comedian.* That staff member who is just waiting to get a quick quip in to show that they really did have a chance at a stand-up career. Nothing better than getting heckled during your presentation.

Lurking variables. What starts as a straightforward conversation on education can swiftly take a turn to left field as staff members' agendas start to arise. Don't get me wrong, this isn't so much of a common occurrence, but I have seen it enough times to consider it part of the pattern. Especially if it is an internal staff member presenting and there is tension amongst staff, a topic can take a sharp turn and suddenly certain colleagues are at each other's throats and about to do 10 steps at dawn.

My consensus is that teachers are considerate beings. Maybe it's that we understand the pressures of what it takes to captivate an audience, or the courage it takes to speak up when you have the chance. One thing is for sure, a whole staff PD will give you a measure of staff morale at any given time.

Tips for Dealing with Stereotypical Staff Members

"We are only as strong as our weakest link." Is a quote I would hear time after time from my coaches over my years involved in team sports. Knowing how to work with team members, what makes them tick, what they need to work on to improve, strengths and weaknesses, all make the process for team growth more efficient.

Here are a few tips I have found useful when working with the characters that arise in a school setting.

The difficult one. The need to talk over people, interrupt conversation, and shoot down new strategies at their inception forms the core of this character. Usually, this colleague has at least a decade of experience and their need to be difficult reflects their disgruntlement with the system. Be wary to not put too much on this colleague at one time or overwhelm them. Remain positive and note the small improvements in a group situation for when this colleague is on the right path.

The insistent talker. A conversation was once described to me as just two people waiting to speak. This colleague makes sure that their time in the spotlight is more consistent than others. Set strict boundaries. I am more than happy to entertain the conversation if the time is right or the situation calls for it, but if you are just talking to talk, this infuriates me. I give one polite warning "Sorry, I just need to get onto this, as time is getting away from me". Usually, the person will get it and move on. If the person then continues, I tell them in a very blunt manner that I need to focus my attention on the task at hand or even throw in a planned ignore occasionally. The key to everything in life is consistency.

The strong silent type. The name says it all. This colleague isn't about the social life in the school. They are here for the job; they usually do the job pretty well and are self-sufficient. The fall back is you will need to put the work in to hunt down or follow up this colleague, but usually they are a good sort and will keep it on the straight and narrow. Let this colleague be. If they need something from you, they will ask and if they don't and they should have, they need to develop that skill further.

The professional. The cream of the crop, the Cadillac of teaching. This colleague understands the importance of professionalism. Firm in their strengths and weaknesses, this colleague will approach any work situation with a level of calm, composure, and confidence. Understanding that teaching is not their be-all and end-all in life, they are able to separate their teaching profession form their self-worth. They understand that there is good days and bad days, and we all experience them, but consistency is the key to stringing more good days together than bad. Let this colleague be.

Trading Horses in the Corral

It takes a special kind of ability to work with behaviour students all day every day. Building relationships, building trust with your students all takes time. Once you get there it is incredible, but the final destination isn't always guaranteed and putting the work in is really the only way to speed up the process.

In saying that, there is the odd colleague or two who would prefer to cut corners and instead of investing time, blood, sweat, and tears, (hypothetical of course, at least the blood part is) will look for the short cut and try to swap students out of their class. Trading names on a class list is what I call it.

The start of the year is a classic example of this. Especially if the staff in your department have been working together for a while and have come to know the students quite well. From the moment the class lists are produced to the staff, the room falls silent, as teachers work over their lists with a fine-tooth comb trying to establish early on how much work the class will be. Teachers start talking about the "superstar" students on their list. Now most teachers will wait a few weeks, hoping that their burst of energy at the start of term from the holiday break will see them through, at least for a few weeks, however a few of your more "difficult" colleagues may try get a jump on the year and fire up then and there.

These are the red flags and patterns of behaviour to look out for from these staff:

They will try to play down the students' they are trying to move real abilities. Look out for sayings like "The student never turns up to my class", or "They have all the natural ability, however, rarely use it". In my experience these are red flags and usually code for "The student never turns up to your class as the relationship you have built with the student is toxic, so they would rather not come to your class". They have the ability, is usually code for "They are bright, and as such, can't wait to sharpen their skills and keep you on your toes."

This student and me have a personality clash. Again, this is another situation where being good at your job in teaching can at times earn you more work if you don't know how to stand up for yourself. Early in my career, I would have elder statesmen (teachers) trying to load me up with their "hard core" students. It almost felt like a natural talent I had of dealing with these students, which it was, but a lot of it came down to observing student behaviour along with building trust and respect.

The student has too much ability or not enough ability for my class. There will be times that this is true, however, there are a lot of times when this will not be true. Knowing that different ability levels exist in your classroom and working to extend these abilities is the hall mark of any good teacher.

If there is a group of students, or even a cohort, which is having problems, somewhere in the year, usually around midyear, there will be a sit down and reshuffle of students. I call this draft day. Teachers involved know this day is coming and have meticulously prepared their notes to get the students they want and keep out the students that will upset their apple cart. Negotiations will start small but as soon as the heavy hitters are on the table (harder students to work with) all sorts of things will be started to be offered up.

End of the day, every student wants someone to believe in them, encourage them, and recognise them for their efforts. Being a professional in the teaching industry should mean that every teacher should aspire to this level for their students.

School Balls

The number one night in a year 12 student's calendar for the year. The ball may be set for later in the year, but you know as soon as day-one of the year comes around, students will be throwing out ideas for how they plan to "attack" the night left, right, and centre.

These are my observations from a teacher's point of view.

The bar is a tricky one. When I was younger it made sense for the bar to be open. Teachers are down on a weekend night giving up their time, of course the majority want to be there, but still, having a drink or two is not the worst thing. These days if I attend the evening I stay away from the bar. Usually, I have driven down and find it hard to stop at one or two, but more I don't believe it is a good look for teachers to be forcing booze down in front of students.

I am not one to be somewhere, just to be somewhere. Most teachers are pretty good like this and will attend the night from start to close. Myself, I try to get there around the main course and stay for a few hours. Usually by this time students have settled, and you can make your way around and talk to individual students. Usually, I will be down for a duty around this time as well, so it keeps the allocated time frame tight.

To this day I think I have been to seven or eight school balls, and I am still not sure of all the duties involved. My go-to move is to try to position myself on door duty during the evening. You get to talk to people as they make their way through, and it is better than walking around a small patch of no-man's land for 60 minutes going crazy. This also beats having to play undercover cop and head and do toilet runs/rotations every 30 minutes to make sure students aren't boozing up.

Then there are the informal duties required. You best make sure as a teacher if you are anywhere in the vicinity of the photo section, you will be hauled in over and over to take photos. Not a bad thing, just make sure you change your poses up or your students will never let you live it down. You must make sure that if you teach any student that is in attendance you have to say hello to them or again, they will never let you live it down. Toilet checks. Make sure you make your way into the toilets every now and again and make sure students aren't trying to smuggle in booze or anything else. Then there is the dance floor. If you can make it to the dance floor for at least one song your memory will be etched in eternal greatness at the school. Well maybe not, but the students will appreciate it.

Finally, teacher dress sense. I have seen it all over my years, my word of advice. Do you. If you are comfortable in it and it is appropriate, go for it.

Meetings

Getting together with colleagues is important. Schools are a collective industry and require feedback from many stakeholders to make sure the best action is chosen heading forward. Running consistent meetings is not necessarily a bad thing. Especially if it is too hard to arrange over email. Staff need to come together to lay down a direction, discuss strategies, and work on solutions. The only problem is it seems more times than not it doesn't go this way.

How schools run their whole-staff meetings will usually say a lot about how the school is run in general. Although I have not been at schools where staff meetings are out of control, I have heard through the "schools' vine" about certain schools; with no one paying attention, people doing their own things and totally ignoring anyone who is presenting. I have been at tougher schools, where the staff meeting can feel like a bull pit at times. Especially for new presenters, getting your material across unscathed by the crowd in attendance can feel like a win for the ages!

To add to the above, the staff room can be a territorial place, sit at the wrong table and you may find yourself upsetting social pressures and seating positions. Rocking up to a whole school staff meeting early to claim your position is a must and where you are sitting is going to say a whole lot about you.

No matter what the meeting is for, the types of characters present at the meeting will always follow a template. This one is classic, especially in smaller run meetings. In my experience I have found most staff will want to say something at one point, especially if the meeting has developed legs and staff are starting to run with it. However, there will always be that one staff member who will talk a little more and attempt to control things if they can have their way. The jokester will usually make an appearance somewhere during a meeting. Devil's advocate, another way to put this is the difficult one will usually make an appearance as well. No matter how well a strategy is developed or put forth, this staff member will find a way to pick holes or offer a counter intuitive suggestion. The silent soldiers. This will be most staff present at this meeting, who only speak when spoken too, listen to all opinions whether they agree or not and will be the ones to deliver on the words spoken once the meeting is complete.

Good luck trying to schedule a meeting with staff members first time round and having everyone agree, sign up, and then rock up. It is not necessarily that staff don't want to catch up, although this can be the case, but with the teaching profession being so short on time, staff cannot always make it on time. I know when I took on year coordinator roles early on in my career, I was all about the meetings. I would become frustrated when more experienced staff would not always rock up or be physically at the meeting and yet would seem soulless when any discussion was attempted. This would drive me insane. Most of the time I would just reassure myself that these colleagues were just older and bitter and were frustrated with the system. Which was true in some instances. Most of the time, however, I can now see that having been in the system for a length of time, you become tired of having meetings to discuss similar things that were possibly making their way around 5 years ago. Good luck trying to schedule a meeting outside of teaching time, especially if you need many teachers to get together. Mention that you may need a colleague or two to arrive 10-15 minutes earlier than usual and I would be watching your back walking to the car park later that afternoon.

Nothing infuriates me more than having meetings just to have meetings. These are usually the meetings that staff try to set up outside of the mandatory meetings that are required and feel like the person running it is just dying to say, "look at me in all my greatness, I am able to call a meeting". I don't know whether colleagues just become use to the sound of their own voice, or they feel they need to conform and have meetings to tick a box, but I assure you, running meetings just for the sake of it is a sure-fire way to frustrate people.

Run meetings for sure, no doubt. Just make sure it has an objective and is being considerate of everyone in attendance's time.

We do it for the Money and Fame...

"Involvement in curriculum design, the opportunity to give back to society, and the holidays". These were the reasons a seasoned and wise colleague once told me he had stayed in teaching for as long as he had. Unfortunately, with everything that happens in a day of teaching, we can easily forget why most of us stepped into teaching in the first place. The money and fame. No, I joke. To give back and help the next generation conquer their fears and reach their dreams.

For me, personally, something that I very much enjoy is the challenging environment that teaching provides, with no two days the same. That is not to say that I still don't have days where I question myself and the amount of challenge that is in the profession, as everything I planned for the lesson starts to take a turn for the worse. It is these days, when I was less experienced, that I would question how I would be able to turn it around, then lo-and-behold the next day the lesson would run smoothly. Also, the dynamic nature of teaching captivates me. There is so much going on at one time it is hard not to walk out of the room some days a little impressed with what you were able to accomplish.

The work-life balance is hard to pass up. Sure, there will be work outside of school times and yes, there is even work to complete on holidays at times, but as your career progresses you can find better ways to handle the workload. This was hard for me at first. I always pride myself in my work ethic and that I will be able to outwork anyone when it comes down to it. My first five years of teaching if I wasn't putting in the hours before and after class and proving to my colleagues that I was a working machine, I saw myself as a failure. Sure, I achieved some things, and more importantly helped my students achieve some things, but it became unsustainable. These days I remind myself that there will always be something to do and make sure to leave the office at a fair time.

I guess it is a no-brainer, but the people you work side by side with daily can have a large effect on your level of work satisfaction. At least, it does for me. Some of the most challenging schools I have worked at, still to this day, the colleges are some of my closest friends. I guess you learn a lot about one another being in the trenches day-in and day-out and you soon learn that if you don't learn to support, and hopefully trust, one another your time can become incredibly stressful and lonely.

Now for the final one and, for most of us out there, the most important one; the opportunity to help people. Helping students overcome their fears and self-limitations is the best feeling for me. Supporting students that were able to persevere and continue to challenge themselves even though they faced trials and tribulations and failures along the way, is the biggest gift we can give the future generations. To learn to keep on getting up even though you have been knocked down, is in my mind the most important skill you can teach someone.

It is crazy to think that almost a decade and a half of teaching has flown past my eyes. There have been the good times and the tough times but during each of these times I wake up each day grateful for what I do.